Loving Nature...

the right way

A Family Guide to Viewing and
Photographing Scenic Areas and Wildlife

Text and Photography By William W. Hartley
Foreword by Leonard Lee Rue, III

Cover Photography

Front Cover Upper Left: Jacqueline van Hartley and a newborn fawn. This interaction should never occur in the wild. Although cute, the depicted situation is unnatural and could endanger the well being of both parties if attempted in the wild. This fawn is being rehabilitated and habituated for a children's petting zoo.C

Front Cover Upper Right: The strength of a nation is often only as strong as its natural resources and its ability to conserve and preserve those resources. The bald eagle, our nation's symbol of strength, was saved from the brink of extinction only through the passing of the Endangered Species Act. Its numbers have grown and its status has been upgraded from endangered to threatened.C

Front Cover Lower Left: Surfacing for just a moment to breathe, the beluga whale returns to the icy depths. Its world remains a mystery to us. C

Front Cover Lower Right: In setting up for a dramatic image depicting what not to do, professional animal trainer Bill Vergis poses as if photographing a wild Kodiak grizzly bear. Even Bill was startled when Buck's sidekick Maney decided to sneak up and join the scene.C

Back Cover Upper Right: Shasha's instinct to explore her natural environment leads her to sniff and taste my standby camera. She is a juvenile timber wolf training to become a professional wildlife model. Ninety-five percent of all published wolf photographs are taken under controlled conditions.C

Back Cover Lower Left: Bow, a habituated rehabilitated endangered species barred owl, is perched as if to illustrate the important relationship between habitat protection and species survival.C

Loving Nature…the right way:
A Family guide to Viewing and Photographing Scenic Areas and Wildlife

Text and Photography by William W. Hartley
Foreword by Leonard Lee Rue, III

First Edition
First Printing, 1996

Book Design: B.P. Imagecraft, Inc. Crystal Lake, Illinois: David B. Bromley
Editorial Team: Senior Editor: Bruce Hopkins; Natural History Editor: Gary Stolz; Copy Editor: Carol J. Kersavage; Legal Review: Paul E. Kennedy; 1st Reader: Robert D. McCall; Final Reader: Judith van Yesseldyk
Image Scanning: Northwoods Personally Yours, Woodruff, Wisconsin
Printed in U.S.A. @ IntraNet Solutions, Inc., Minneapolis, Minnesota

Library of Congress
Cataloging–in–Publication Data

Hartley, William W., 1957
    Loving Nature … the right way: A Family Guide to Viewing and Photographing Scenic Areas and Wildlife – 1st ed.
            Includes index
            ISBN 1-888859-00-8
                1. Nature Photography – Adult/General   2. Nature & Natural
History – Adult General
    I. Photography, Loving Nature   II. Title.

Earth is home to all living things—microorganisms, amphibians, reptiles, plants, fishes, birds and mammals. We are all neighbors and relatives.

Humans share a spiritual bond with other species on Earth. We sense that when we listen to waves crashing on the beach, when we smell a blooming flower, and when we observe a bird in flight.

Photography helps us to better know, understand, and appreciate this spiritual link. The camera is a tool we use to explore our planet. With it we can record species and preserve nature in another form.

Leica Camera, Inc., has made a strong commitment to be part of the solution in protecting the environment. We have joined forces with the Outdoor Writers Association, the National Audubon Society, the New Jersey Audubon Society and the Wildlife Conservation Society to help build a better tomorrow.

We also have made adjustments and modifications within our company to help protect the environment. We have replaced plastic packaging materials with recyclable cardboard. We use CKW-free cleaning agents during manufacturing, and all leather cases for cameras, lenses and binoculars are made of PCB-free tanned leather. Our brochures are printed on paper bleached without chlorine and consisting of environmentally friendly pigments. Our office recycles all paper, glass, and aluminum. Thus, Leica Camera now meets and/or exceeds all of U.S. environmental protection laws.

We are proud to sponsor this book. Leica has a worldwide reputation as a technological leader. It is our goal to become a leader in environmental protection and understanding as well. We believe it is our responsibility to help preserve the natural world. By preserving it, we also preserve our pleasure in it.

Cheryl Van Sise
Leica Camera, Inc.

Bogen Photo Corporation, a distributor of fine photographic and cine/video equipment has environmentally conscious ties that go back to our founder. Lester H. Bogen's personal darkroom featured a state-of-the-art disposal system at a time when most people were unaware of the need to consider the proper handling of chemicals.

We are proud to say that this tradition is carried on today as Bogen Photo Corporation and its affiliated manufacturers continue to exercise ways to reduce environmental waste. Our equipment is carefully engineered to offer the greatest flexibility and durability even under the most demanding outdoor conditions. Many of the features stem from our willingness to listen to our customers and our commitment to respond.

It is said that luck is the result of proper preparation. Although we offer a wide selection of photographic and cine/video equipment, there is one thing missing that we can't offer: your creative vision.

Lorenzo E. Gasperini
Bogen Photo Corporation

Acknowledgements

In writing and photographing this guide, I have received much help, advice, and useful information from many people, companies, associations, and societies.

I would especially like to thank the following for their help and contributions: Agfa Film; Roger Archibald, Environmental Writer / Photographer; Bruce Batten, Public Affairs, U.S. Fish and Wildlife Service; Dan and Pam Bacon, Red Feather Lake Photo Center; Bruce Blank, American Society of Media Photography; Bogen Photo Corp.; Don and Karen Bonica, Toms River Avian Care; Gary Braasch, Photographer / Writer; Bureau of Land Management, U.S. Department of the Interior; Cape May County Zoo; John DeCock, Associate Director of Conservation, Sierra Club; Susan Colclazer, Chief of Interpretation, Bryce Canyon National Park; Tom L. Darden, National Wildlife Program Manager, USDA Forest Service; Sandra Snell-Dobert, Norris District Naturalist, Yellowstone National Park; Eastman Kodak Company; Mike Finley, Superintendent, Yellowstone National Park; Karen Wade, Superintendent, Great Smoky Mountains National Park; Don Gascon; Wayne C. Grieme; Fran Hacket, Public Relations, New York Aquarium; Louis S. Hinds, III, Refuge Manager, J.N. "Ding" Darling National Wildlife Refuge; Kurt Hofer and sons, Vienna; Ikelite Underwater Systems; Interagency Grizzly Bear Committee, U.S. Forest Service; Lyle Jensen, New England Alive, Inc.; Dan Johnson, Naturalist Interpreter, Olympic National Park; Kevin Johnson, Ranger, Denali National Park; Ken Kehrer, Jr., Chief Ranger, Denali National Park; Paul E. Kennedy, Esq.; Roger Kennedy, Director, National Park Service; Leica Camera, Inc.; George Lepp, Photographer / Writer; Elaine Leslie, Wildlife Biologist, Grand Canyon National Park; Ricardo Lewis, Visual Information Specialist, National Park Service; Larry Lofton, Attleboro National Hatchery; Mark J. Lukes, President, North American Nature Photography Association; Nancy Marx, Division of Refuges, U.S. Fish and Wildlife Service; Robert McCall, Photographer / Writer; National Park Service, U.S. Department of the Interior; New Jersey Aquarium: Thea Nordling, Chief of Interpretation, Denali National Park; John Nuhn, Photo Editor, National / International Wildlife Magazines; Theodore Ondler, Editor / Publisher, Photo Traveler; Jim Rainey, Executive Director, Outdoor Writers Association of American; Jeanne Rayser, Woodford Cedar Run Wildlife Refuge; Dr. Leonard Lee Rue, III. Photographer / Naturalist / Writer; Len Rue, Jr., Photographer / Writer; Robert J. Shallenberger, Chief, Division of Refuges, U.S. Fish and Wildlife Service; Helen Longest-Slaughter, Natural History Photojournalist; Gary W. Stanley, Photographer / Tour Leader; Gary M. Stolz, National Education and Training Center, U.S. Fish and Wildlife Service; The U.S. Fish and Wildlife Service; Bill Vergis, Jungleworld; The Wildlife Conservation Society.

A very special thanks to my wife Marleen, who supported and encouraged me through many long and irregular hours with much understanding, patience and practical help.

This book is dedicated to the
loving memory of my sister,
Sandra M. Hartley (1956-1994),
who died of breast cancer.

Contents

A photographic image traditionally has been perceived as a truthful portrayal of reality. That may have been close to the truth in photography's infancy but not today. Like most wildlife photographers, I use various resources in creating my photography. I work most often in the wild, but I also work with animal and bird rehabilitation centers, zoos, aquariums, endangered species reentry programs and wildlife models. Note: Each photograph in this book is marked with either a "C" indicating that the image was taken under controlled conditions or a "W" meaning the image was taken in the wild.

Foreword

William "Bill" Hartley's book is an idea whose time has come.

Long before Earth Day originated in 1970, I was an interpretive naturalist conducting outdoor education classes introducing thousands of young people to the intimacies of nature that I grew up living among and loving. This coincided with the tremendous upsurge in the interest in everything having to do with the out-of-doors, a time when people everywhere wanted to "get back to nature." But the environment in many areas could not withstand the onslaught of the numerous people that descended on it. People, not figuratively but actually, "loved to death" the plants, birds, animals, and the land itself.

In my classes I could caution the students about the frailty of nature and teach them how to relate to it without destroying it. Unfortunately, there were hundreds of thousands of people who had bought hiking boots, backpacks, birding binoculars, and perhaps a camera and telephoto lenses. They stormed the out-of-doors without any real knowledge of, or regard for, the wild world they were entering. This was not done with malice aforethought; it was the result of simply not knowing. It is for that reason and for those people that this book is written. We all can learn from *Loving Nature...the right way.*

Bill Hartley is in the right place at the right time to do the job. He has a degree in resources development from the University of Rhode Island, but the degree is merely an extension and expansion of his lifelong love affair with nature. He spent most of his childhood and school years living on the edge of New Jersey's Pine Barrens. If ever a place was misnamed, it is the coastal region of southern New Jersey known as the Barrens. According to the dictionary, barren means devoid of plant and animal life. Nothing could be further from the truth about the Pine Barrens. Bill lived on the edge of one of nature's great ecological laboratories. The Barrens has vegetation so thick it is all but impassable in many areas. It teems with birds and other animals. It has many plants that are rare or not found at all anywhere else in the world. Spending his formative years in such an environment gave him a grounding in all of nature that cannot be learned from schools or books.

To help those who have not had the opportunity to have had this constant exposure to nature and its ways, Bill is sharing his knowledge through this book.

Many of my students, most of whom lived in the city, often asked, "What can I do to help protect the environment?" There were many things they could do, some as simple as "Don't litter," "Don't pick the wildflowers," "Don't disturb birds and their nests," "Don't harass wildlife," "Volunteer to clean up the environment," "Join and support such organizations as the National Wildlife Federation, National Audubon Society, and the Sierra Club." All of these ideas—and a lot more—are covered in this book.

Each year a number of people are injured by wildlife in many of our natural areas. Many act out of a lack of knowledge or from misinformation about the creatures they want to see. Folks forget they are guests at the homes of the wildlife they are watching or attempting to photograph. They do things they would not do as guests in another human's home. This book is basically about wildlife etiquette. Civilization is nothing more than large numbers of people trying to live in harmony with one another, respecting each other's individuality, guided by what we call laws that spell out what is considered the right and wrong ways to act. This book is a guide, or a handbook, on how to get along with nature without harming the wildlife or putting yourself in a position to be harmed.

Bill draws not only on his own expertise but the expertise of many trained, highly regarded people who cover the entire spectrum of knowledge about natural history. Each of their essays is a pearl of wisdom.

You would not think of going on a trip without a road map to guide you on your way. You should not think of starting out on your adventures with scenic areas and wildlife without a map. Bill's book is your road map to knowledge and pleasure in the out-of-doors. Bon voyage!

Dr. Leonard Lee Rue, III

As I walked the main trail behind the Mirror Lake Visitor Center in Glacier National Park, I came upon this mountain goat and scenic view. Most parks are home to any wildlife species.

W

Part One: Of Dreams and Memories

Loving Nature to Death

"We have found our enemy and he is us."
—Pogo

Viewing and photographing wildlife is not about watching or photographing nature and animals. It is about living our dreams. And conservation is not about saving this species or that species. It is about saving those dreams.

Most people truly are concerned about the plight of whales, eagles, and bears without ever having seen one in the wild, but they dream of the time they might meet one. Our imaginations become alive with escapes from reality as we revisit our roots and dream of a more natural world, of places where wild beasts we have met only through films, photographs, and words, roam freely. We take comfort in knowing they still have natural homes, and we wait to fulfill our dreams of experiencing wild places and seeing wild animals.

If it had not been for the dreams, wisdom, and passion of a few of our forefathers who created the national park, national forest, and national wildlife refuge systems, today's parklands would not exist. These few people believed, as many do today, that a species is entitled to exist for its own sake, and they made the assumption that each life form may prove valuable in a way we cannot yet understand or measure.

Our remaining shrinking natural areas offer sanctuary not only to many wild creatures but to humans. We visit natural areas in increasing numbers to escape urban pressures and to enjoy encounters with nature. Last year alone more than 500 million visits were made to national parks and wildlife refuges throughout the United States and Canada. But with a ratio of one ranger to approximately every 85,000 visitors, it is impossible to educate, guide, and inform even a small percentage of those following their dreams to remote wilderness lands. Natural area managers cannot properly handle the increasing stream of dreamers. As visitors, we come, we see, we experience, and we go home. The plants and animals are home.

We truly are having a hard time protecting our ever-shrinking wild ecosystems because of the pressures put on them by industry and our growing population. Even the places we have set aside, such as the national parks and wildlife refuges, are damaged by well-meaning visitors who are in many ways loving nature to death.

Our remaining places of beauty and wonder fill the pages of popular magazines. Travel guides tell us how to get there and where to go when we arrive, but few tell us how to enjoy these areas and their inhabitants without causing further harm. We tend to exclude ourselves from the natural world. Instead, we think of environmental pressures on a grand scale: development, pollution, industry, human population and habitat loss. But wildlife and environmental pressures come in all sizes and forms. An issue that has been addressed the least, our personal interaction with the natural world, is the easiest and simplest to control.

Just like you, I consider myself truly concerned about nature, but when we venture into a natural area it never dawns on us that we may not be doing the right thing in the eyes of the natural world. Nature has its own unwritten rules by which it governs itself, a system alien to most well-meaning visitors.

If no one sees me do it, then it is all right. Who cares? Society says it is all right to take a shortcut around that turn or walk across that grass. Look at almost any college campus or business park in the suburban United States; each is riddled with dirt shortcuts etched in fields of green. Shortcuts are not necessarily acceptable in the natural world. My memories are haunted by them:

I love the feeling of sand as it washes out from under my feet with the retreat of each wave, of building sand castles, and of collecting shells. But most of all I love the giggling sounds of my daughter as she races back and forth up the beach with the rhythmic motion of the crashing waves.

Last summer, while I was inspecting a tern colony in a closed area on Long Beach Island, New Jersey, as a participant in New Jersey's Endangered Species Program, I came upon some footprints in the sand. They were created by someone who had obviously ignored the "closed" sign and picked up the rope, ducked under, and proceeded to take a shortcut to the ocean. I followed these prints until I came upon what used to be a tern's nest. The nest had consisted of a scratch in the sand with three tiny eggs, each no bigger than a nickel. Soon the wind would blow, filling in that single footprint and covering those three broken eggs that soon would have become baby birds.

This endangered species, least tern hatchling, no larger than a nickel, blends in extremely well with its surroundings on Long Beach Island, New Jersey. Because of our inability to see and pick out eggs and hatchlings in the sand, management teams often close off colony areas. W

My first trip to Yosemite National Park provoked a variety of mixed emotions. The vast, spectacular majestic landscapes were breathtaking, but the details surrounding these areas made me ill. Well-meaning visitors had riddled the landscapes—the very scenic areas that had drawn us there in the first place—with a patchwork of paths.

One of the most frightening incidents I have witnessed took place in Yellowstone National Park about six years ago. My wife and I were traveling the park's east road that leads toward Mammoth Hot Springs when we spotted a bear far off in the valley below. I quickly mounted an 800mm lens onto a tripod hoping to get a better look and maybe an image or two. My camera drew a crowd and within a few minutes we had what the rangers affectionately refer to as a "bear jam," a stream of cars blocking the road. Car doors slammed, radios blasted, people shouted and pointed from the far side of the U-shaped road nearly a quarter mile away. The air hummed with comments: "A bear, isn't he cute!" "I want to get closer." The bear was not a he at all, but a she, a sow grizzly with two tiny cubs—a scenario for the worst possible human–bear encounter.

I cannot understand why someone would want to confront a wild animal that could pick him up, shred him with one swat of its claws, and eat him. But there, out of the corner of my eye, I spotted a man with a boy about 10 years old heading down the adjacent slope toward the bears to get a closer look at the "cute, fuzzy, lovable" bears. My heart jumped into my throat and my mind raced as I started across the meadow to intercept and stop a possible tragedy from occurring. Thank God, a park ranger came from out of nowhere and stopped the sightseers.

I do not mind that I was not the first and only person to climb to the crest of Mount Margaret in Denali National Park, but I love the memory of the view of Mount McKinley and of the Dall's ram, marmot, ptarmigan, caribou, golden eagle, ground squirrel, and grizzly bear that were there to greet me.

By using an 800 mm lens, I created the effect of being only feet away from this Dall's ram, when in fact I am on an adjacent ridge more than 100 feet away in Denali National Park. W

I also love sitting at a campfire and listening to the bittersweet cry of a lone wolf as its voice fills the empty night sky, the distant whoo–whoo–whooing of the great horned owl, the peeep–peeep–peeping of the spring peeper, and the not-too-distant whipper of the whip–poor–will as the mint green leaves of spring shine silver under a midnight moon.

Many folks do not seem to understand that wild animals are wild. Many people seem to want to get up close to wildlife as if they were visiting zoos instead of national parks, refuges, and forests. When wild animals lose their fear of humans, resource managers are forced to either destroy the animals or move them farther into the backcountry, thereby reducing our opportunities of viewing them.

Few persons have had the pleasure and excitement of encountering a school of hammerhead sharks. The ocean teams with life off Darwin Island. W

I love the sensation of entering the unknown. When I rolled out of a ponga, a small diving skiff, off the islands of Darwin and Wolf in the Galapagos, I entered into a new world of cobalt blue teeming with more than 250 hammerhead sharks. As I drifted silently downward into the vast emptiness, the shadows came to life in perfect synchronization. Effortlessly they propelled themselves swiftly forward and passed within only a few feet of me.

I have had similar experiences in the waters off the Channel Islands, off Cape Cod, in Puget Sound and elsewhere. I also have had such experiences spoiled by jet skiers as they came over the horizon pounding the surf on their new toys. In stark contrast to these noise makers, ocean-going kayaks glide gracefully through the waters off Newfoundland and Acadia National Park. Yet, even these silent, elegant, low-impact communes with nature may have a detrimental impact as marine species are forced off their feeding and resting grounds.

One of the great victories born out of the environmental crusade of the 1970s is that whale watching has replaced commercial whaling and we have traded in our harpoons and ropes for cameras and binoculars. Although whalers no longer ply their trade in the traditional sense, the new multi-billion dollar industry of whale watching applies a constant pressure on whales and our other aquatic neighbors.

I love sitting on the edge of a bay, lake, pond or stream with my feet dangling in the water as I doze off to the monotonous, repetitive sound of water lapping against the embankment. But sometimes a motorboat roars by and snaps me out of my reverie. My annoyance is minor compared to what the boat's wake and noise might be doing to the marshlands that serve as prolific breeding grounds and nurseries for aquatic and terrestrial creatures. Are these places playgrounds without boundaries or rules, places where motorboats can churn silted bottoms and pulverize marine vegetation? Should jet skis be allowed to terrorize the abundant life in shallow-water mud flats and coves and along salt marshes, streams, tributaries, and other areas traditionally off-limits to motorized watercraft?

Nutrient-rich waters the color of pea-green soup are nourished by millions of microorganisms. But in chocolate–brown, silt-laden waters, bivalves choke, smother and suffocate. Pelagic, bottom–dwelling and filter-feeder fish, along with all kinds of ducks and other birds are driven from their habitat.

There are too many people and too few wild places. Everybody wants his own little piece. Limited as these may be, our country's natural areas still offer spectacular vistas and unique and pristine ecosystems rich with biodiversity. These lands provide home and shelter for an incredible number of wild creatures. More than 700 bird species, 250 reptiles and amphibians, at least 200 mammals, 200 types of fish and thousands of invertebrates, plants and microorganisms are there for us to discover.

Each time I traverse America's heartland and gaze over fields of swaying grain, I dream of a time before European settlers cast their shadows upon these lands. I imagine a time when my father's father's father walked these lands and lived in harmony with nature.

Countless moons have passed since our great plains were seas of grass that roared with the thunder of great herds of buffalo moving from one feeding ground to another or when the skies were blackened with the migrations of millions of waterfowl and our northern rivers boiled with annual parades of salmon swimming upstream. We have altered much of our planet, forgotten much of our past, and understand little of what is left.

Stewardship in Nature Photography

"Just a little closer for a full frame." How many times has this thought crossed our minds as we trample through vegetation, step off the trail, and drive off the road to get just a little closer to take a photograph? How many times have we made noise to cause our subject to turn toward us or even put ourselves in potentially dangerous situations until we frighten a wild animal and it bolts to safety, its heart racing with adrenaline? Yes, even if unintentional, we do have an impact on the very animals and habitats we love, admire, and travel distances to see.

All of us care about the wildlife we view and photograph or we would not be out there lugging all that expensive and heavy equipment through the heat and cold, mud and mosquitoes, just to take home more pictures. However, there is a deeper meaning. Our pictures reveal wonderful memories of being in touch with nature's beauty. We see rare and endangered species as indicators of biodiversity and vanishing ecosystems. They remind us of our need to protect important and ever-shrinking wildlife habitats and ecosystems that we, too, share.

As we humans continue our time bomb of exponential population growth, habitat destruction, and pollution of our environment, more and more of us seek to escape the stress of our complex lives through solitude and a return to our species' past. Nature photography is a wonderful, healthy, and educational way to explore and meet these basic human needs. Through nature photography we also can educate others to understand, appreciate, and protect the natural world.

How our needs are met in ways compatible with protecting the very habitats and species we love is the subject of this book. Only by fostering long-range stewardship of natural places will our children and grandchildren have wildlife treasures to enjoy.

Gary M. Stolz
National Education and Training Center
U.S. Fish & Wildlife Service

The industrial revolution and global human population explosion have altered forever wildlife habitats and delicately balanced ecosystems of which we, too, are a part. With the European discovery of this bountiful land came dreams of riches, a new world to be conquered and subdued. Soon pockets of civilization sprouted up in the wilderness, swelled, and took over immense areas. Civilization spread like the plague, consuming vast quantities of both flora and fauna. In less than 500 years, more than 500 species and subspecies of plants and animals became extinct at the hands of man.

American bison were reduced in numbers from an estimated 60 million to fewer than 300 individuals, and only one of three subspecies remains. Tales passed down from early settlers tell of passenger pigeons filling woodland forests and masses of Labradorian ducks floating on northern currents. Both species have disappeared forever from our planet.

Our nation's wild habitats are shrinking. Today, less than two percent of our continent's tall grass prairies remains intact from the ravages of domestic livestock or the plow. Of our old-growth forest, less than three percent still stands. And nothing more than a drop in a bucket remains unaltered or uncontaminated of our nation's most fertile natural habitats—the wetlands. As natural ecosystems are diminished or destroyed, wildlife dwindles or disappears. Today, more than 900 species are recognized as either endangered or threatened and more than 3,700 species are waiting for official recognition of their endangered status.

We have lost our ability to converse with nature, to see ourselves as part of it, and to understand the natural world as our ancestors did before us. Animals and other forms of nature taught us survival, helped us develop behavior patterns, and perhaps etched the blueprint for our ability to think. How can we hunt without being hunted, eat without being eaten? Animals showed us when fruits and nuts were ripe and which buds and sprouts were safe to consume. They led us to shelter and wintering grounds and taught us about environmental interactions and limitations. They fed and clothed us.

In our lives, endangered species are the proverbial canary in the mine shaft. Even with the unexplainable disappearance of so many songbirds and amphibians worldwide, we continue digging the shaft deeper. We fail to see endangered species as messengers proclaiming that something is out of balance and our survival is at stake.

I sometimes dream of a time when the cure for cancer or AIDS is found not buried deep in the heart of some remote jungle or at the depths of a bottomless ocean but locked up inside the life forces of every plant, animal, insect, and microorganism. I dream of a cure in the sum of all living things.

At its height, the bison population in America neared sixty million. Now as silhouettes of a bygone era, small herds roam the National Bison Range in Montana and a few other parks and preserves. W

When that day comes, the land barons, industrial tycoons and greed mongers will scramble to salvage all they have destroyed. The redemption will not be done in an act of kindness or for the good of their fellow man but to increase their bottom line.

Mankind's greatest challenge, the need to preserve our planet and all that lives on it, lies before us. Will we make a conscious effort for the good of all? Have we, in our quest for everyone's rights, forgotten our responsibilities? Or will we go on abusing and exploiting the natural world?

I do not pretend to have the answers. I am not even sure what the right questions are, but I know extinction is forever and education is the key to unlocking closed minds and the doors to our past.

With a single pen stroke, a decision is rendered and a verdict pronounced. Morals, legislation, dollars and greed determine which species shall live and which shall die. I dream of a time when every creature is granted the right to exist, a right not based on the fact it might hold the cure for cancer, just a right to live.

I may be dreaming, but I know one thing for sure: I love knowing that as an individual I can, and will, make a difference.

Obedience to the Unenforceable

The consideration of ethical conduct never has been a simple matter. With each generation, each cultural or religious revolution, and each technological advancement, our ethical standards have evolved. Wars have been fought and civilizations have disappeared because of differences in moral and ethical beliefs.

It is no wonder that as we discuss the ethics of nature photography there is little agreement and lots of controversy. In trying to explain ethics to my 9-year-old, I said, "Ethics means doing what you know is right even when no one is watching." In making presentations to photographers, I define ethics as "obedience to the unenforceable." Using either definition, one thing becomes obvious—there is no way to legislate or police ethical behavior.

Numerous ethical dilemmas face nature photographers. Should we support the photography of captive or controlled animals? Is a computer-manipulated nature photograph really a natural history photograph? Should editors caption photos as having come from game farms or having been digitally altered? How does computer manipulation differ from Ansel Adams altering his famous "Moonrise Over Hernandez" in the darkroom? Although each of us may have a response to these questions, none of us has the answers.

It is not critical, nor is it possible, that we agree on every specific ethical concern. What is important is that we find a common thread that may serve to instill a general sense of ethical conduct in the field. That common thread is knowledge. The more each of us learns about our environment and the wildlife we photograph, the easier it will be to make ethical choices as we pursue our passion and our livelihood through nature photography.

Mark J. Lukes
President
North American Nature Photography Association

*Do not approach a wild bear under any circumstances. These Kodiak grizzlys settling their differences were photographed with a 400 mm lens and a 1.4 extender, creating, in effect, a 600 mm lens. The bears were photographed from over 200 feet away.*C

Stewardship in Nature Photography

Be Aware About Wildlife

We humans love wildlife. Unfortunately, we love wildlife to death. In many of our parks and remaining wild places, our presence has an adverse impact on the very animals that draw us near.

In our national parks, which draw visitors from around the world, the feeding, touching, and harassment of wildlife are prohibited by federal law. These actions threaten the survival of park animals. Losing their fear of humans and becoming habituated to unnatural food sources leads to a chain reaction of sometimes fatal events: animals quickly learn to frequent roadsides to beg for food, and often these animals are injured or killed by cars.

If the cars do not get them, the junk food will. The various components of human foods lead to the deterioration of the health of wildlife. The animals become dependent on human food sources and eventually decrease natural foraging behavior. Habituation can be deadly, not only for wildlife, but also for humans. Although they appear to be quite docile, almost tame, wild animals are capable of inflicting serious harm to people.

What can you do to ensure your safety and that of the wildlife you wish to observe? Be aware! If an animal's normal behavior is interrupted, you are too close. When driving, always allow animals to cross unobstructed and remember that animals quite often move in pairs or groups. Keep alert! If one deer crosses the road, more are likely to follow. Park only in turnouts. Sudden stops to view wildlife only cause traffic jams, accidents, and flaring tempers.

Use binoculars or a telephoto lens for your observations, so you can enjoy wildlife while observing their normal behavior and ensuring their safety and yours. Never approach wildlife! Many wild animals have become used to the approach of humans. Keep a safe distance. Should an animal respond to your approach by flight or fight, it is often too late for a speedy retreat, and serious injury, even death, may result.

Never feed wildlife! Animals' digestive systems are not suited for the consumption of human foods. They quickly will become habituated to unhealthy foods and quite often consume the packaging as well. This almost always results in the slow, prolonged death of the animal.

Be prepared! When planning your trip or upon entry into a park, inquire at a ranger station or visitor center about the best locations for observing wildlife. Make yourself aware of what laws and regulations pertain to wildlife in the area. Local experts can provide interesting information about what species to look for and about seasonal behavior of animals.

As a visitor, remember wildlife is a resource and it is the responsibility of each of us to protect this resource. Realize that the greatest wildlife experience is the opportunity to view wildlife being wild!

Elaine Leslie
Wildlife Biologist
Grand Canyon National Park

Our Big Backyard

"Of what avail is an open eye if the heart is blind."
—Solomon Ibn-Gabirol

On a still afternoon in late fall I stumbled upon a den. A lingering scent revealed its location. The aroma seemed like that of a skunk, only less pungent. Looking around, then following my nose, I was led down a slight embankment adjacent to a clearing in the forest. At the bottom of the slope was a burrow. Surrounding tracks and scat indicated this den was being used by a fox family.

The temperature was warm. Golden-yellow and rust orange leaves rustled in a slight breeze. Dew from the night's mist covered all the vegetation and the smell of decaying leaves rose from the forest floor.

Some 30 days later I again was sitting outside the den at dawn. The seasons had changed since my first visit. The crystal-clear sky was a cobalt blue, and autumn's pastel colors had been replaced by muted grays and browns with occasional patches of deep forest green. A light snow had fallen, the first of the winter season, and the ground was covered with a few inches of soft, cold, white powder. The air seemed especially cold and damp. Tree branches

Patience is more often than not the key ingredient to successfully viewing and photographing predators and prey, simply because wild animals have no schedule or appointments to keep. C

Although my daughter has been close to wildlife, she has never been this close to a wild animal because of the potential danger involved. This fawn had lost its mother to an automobile accident

sparkled. With each breath I exhaled, a trail of vapor rose in the morning light.

Day after day I arrived before sunrise and quietly entered my blind by taking the long way around so as not to be seen or smelled. Early on several mornings I glimpsed the fox carrying food back to her den, but there was little visible activity, for foxes generally are nocturnal. Usually by 9:30 a.m. I had finished my photography and was heading back to the office.

On one particular morning, the hum from commuters' cars on the highway grew louder as the sun rose. I wondered whether I could obtain good photos. For five consecutive mornings I had inched my blind a little closer to the den until I was within range with a 5.6/800mm lens. Now, 50 days since discovering the den, the weather was getting even colder and daylight shorter. I knew I could not spend much more time trying to get photos.

A vehicle's horn drew my attention to the roadway. I caught a glimpse of something approaching. Swinging the camera around and focusing on the approaching fox, I noticed something in its mouth. I needed quick work and luck to get a good shot. An animal approaching head-on is very difficult to photograph with a manual focusing camera system. Four quick exposures and she was gone.

After the fox was back in her den, it was time to pack up the portable blind and leave. For a month my blind had sat unmolested within earshot of a major thoroughfare. Most people were insulated, isolated, and cocooned in their cars. Few of them ventured out into this patch of woods.

I loaded my gear into the back of my pickup. Traffic was light because nearly everyone was heading to work in the other direction. It was only a 15-minute drive to my office. Then I noticed a dead deer on the roadside, a dangerous place for vultures to feast.

Adrenaline still pumping from the excitement of my close encounter with the fox, I thought of how much wildlife could be photographed around my home and in other urban habitats throughout the world. This past spring I photographed a newborn fawn and its mother feeding on flowers in my backyard. My daughter, not yet two years old, would wave from the back porch deck and say, "Good morning, deer."

On a number of occasions the deer would allow her to approach; no one else, only Jacqueline. Those were precious moments, etched forever in my memory. I would sit, smiling, with my camera and long lens mounted on a tripod and photograph two young souls, untethered by prejudice and peers, meeting and exchanging a purity of ultimate understanding and love. Ah, such innocence.

*and was being hand-raised to go to a petting zoo. Even with deer and daughter in the field of flowers, it took the better part of a day for the two to decide to come together on their own.*C

Then I thought about all the large wading birds in the small pond next to my parents' place in Florida and of the armadillo that feeds on insects in their backyard.

Thoughts came back of a visit in Southern California with Bob McCall photographing coyotes from his back door and sea lions from the harbor pier and of walking with Paul Kennedy and his daughter, Tara, in Massachusetts and spotting a salamander crossing the sidewalk and a tree frog climbing their garage door. I

As I drifted patiently along in the currents of a nutrient-rich water column off New Jersey, an ocean sunfish, one of the world's largest bony fish, appeared from out of the murky depths. W

recalled seeing great horned owls and broad-winged hawks in urban cemeteries. I remembered a small town in Texas where I photographed prairie dogs and burrowing owls in the town square, and I mused about photographing a mule deer behind a Midwestern elementary school.

My daydreaming was interrupted by the sight of a red-tailed hawk sitting in a tree in the median of the road. The hawk was feeding on a freshly caught mouse but looked up as a car with a noisy muffler passed in the other lane. Red-tailed hawks often feed along grassy road embankments and return to the same perch to roost or hunt, so cars make perfect portable photo blinds.

Upon returning home, I found six wild turkeys enjoying cracked corn by the bird feeder. Over the months they had grown accustomed to the truck and only glanced up. Grabbing my camera gear and tripod, I entered the house through the garage and went directly to the dining room window. I set up my camera, slowly opened the window to reduce the glare from the glass, and took two or three frames. Then the phone rang and brought me back to reality. Another assignment: a photographic/text essay on underwater New Jersey.

No kidding, New Jersey! You no doubt have never heard anything good about New Jersey's coastal waters. What, you wonder, could possibly live in an ocean that sometimes looks like pea soup? The Jersey shore has an undeserved unfavorable reputation. Unbeknownst to the general public, this state's coastal waters are highly prolific. The nutrient-rich ocean teems with life. The entire water column from surface to subsand offers incredible opportunities to find magnificent creatures, some so small they are visible only with a microscope while others are larger than humans.

Although New Jersey's coastal biological diversity may be more limited than tropical waters, the populations of each species are greater. Ocean–dwelling species feed on small fish and invertebrates. The more territorial species, however, search for oases created by artificial reefs, sunken ships, and sand drifts. Below the lapping surface of waves, a beauty and poetic elegance are created by the ocean's perpetual motion. I can hardly wait to start that new assignment.

What a day! Sometimes I have traveled to exotic distant parts of the world and have seen less than right in my own backyard and in my extended backyard, the community. We do not have to travel to the ends of the Earth to find scenic areas and wildlife to fulfill our dreams and provoke our memories. They are all around us.

Watchable Wildlife

How do we meet the needs of millions of people who have a passion for nature and wildlife and who want to observe or photograph wildlife in natural habitats?

This was one of many important questions asked at a meeting of the federal and state agencies and private conservation organizations in February 1989. These conservation professionals saw the writing on the wall; there was an intense and growing public interest in pursuing wildlife-viewing opportunities, a demand not being met.

A strategy was needed to bring groups together to establish a national network of wildlife viewing areas, to provide associated educational opportunities, and to get people actively involved in wildlife and habitat conservation. It was critically important these opportunities satisfied both the public's needs for experiencing wildlife and the agencies' needs for ensuring a quality experience without adverse impacts to the wildlife and their habitats.

And so, through a partnership agreement signed by all the federal land-managing agencies, the International Association of Fish and Wildlife Agencies, and four private conservation organizations, the National Watchable Wildlife Program was born. It is envisioned by all who have worked so hard to implement an effective program that viable populations of fish and wildlife species and their habitats will be maintained by building an effective, well-informed constituency for conservation.

To date, more than 28 statewide Watchable Wildlife viewing guides have been developed to help millions of people observe wildlife close to their homes and to lessen the impact on our already overburdened parks and wildlife refuges. Four successful National Watchable Wildlife Conferences have been conducted to help both the agencies and the public find ways to ensure quality experiences. Numerous partnerships have been developed where hard work and a passion for wildlife bring people throughout the world a little closer to realizing and fulfilling our stewardship responsibility.

The fact that you have picked up this book shows your commitment to this responsibility, and the next time you see the brown and white binoculars symbol of the Watchable Wildlife Program, you will know many are working hard to ensure quality viewing experiences.

Nancy Marx
Division of Refuges
U.S. Fish and Wildlife Service

A Last Frontier

"Only to the white man was nature a wilderness and only to him was the land 'infested' with 'wild' animals and 'savage' people. To us it was tame. Earth was bountiful and we were surrounded with the blessing of the Great Mystery."
—Chief Luther Standing Bear
of the Oglala Sioux

Understanding an animal's behavior and anticipating its every move greatly increases your chances of capturing an image. I had seen this hoary marmot the day before tucked between rock ledges, quietly soaking in the mid-day Alaskan sun. W

Kuwatuhena elaihosihtit aesisak. At first I thought it was the whisper of the wind blowing softly through the spruce forest, but it grew louder. *Kuwatuhena elaihosihtit aesisak.* The hairs on the back of my neck were now standing on end, and my blood ran cold. Was I so tired my mind was starting to play tricks on me or was this merely an echo of a distant memory, a lost thought bouncing off some imaginary plane in the depths of my mind? But the wind sang louder, in an ancient tongue, one that I had not heard since my childhood: *Kuwatuhena elaihosihtit aesisak.*

It had been a long couple of weeks, 25 days to be exact, since I left my home in southeastern New Jersey. Days filled with climbing mountains in search of sure-footed Dall sheep; traversing tundra looking for the elusive caribou, moose, grizzly bear, and wolf; laughing at the born-to-be eaten arctic ground squirrels and marmots as they scurried about; repelling rock-faced shorelines in search of towering colonies of kittiwakes and puffins; riding ocean currents with sea lions and seals; and swimming rivers in search of an image of a migrating sockeye salmon.

I had been working from sunrise to sunset, and that does not leave much time for sleeping, especially in a land where the sun never seems to set during the summer.

Alaska's long exhausting summer days make up for the short growing season. With the onset of a spring thaw, plants quickly leave dormancy to flower. Their blossoms turn to berries. The berries ripen to be eaten and create another generation of plants, replenishing the earth. Each plant returns to dormancy a couple of months later. The sun's long summer light generates lifeblood into the tundra flora, the base of the food chain. These plants ultimately feed every animal, both large and small, directly and indirectly. They replenish and nourish, then build up a fatty layer necessary to carry each animal species through as much as nine months of deep freeze.

At the upper reaches of North America, the sun looks very much like a big bouncing ball at the height of the growing season. It touches the horizon and then, never dipping out of sight, starts its return back into the sky. Beautiful long rays of light fill endless days with just the right lighting necessary for great photography.

Kuwatuhena elaihosihtit aesisak hushed the wind, now more clearly than before. But something else caught my attention. In a cavernous hollow, tucked deep in the night shadows of the surrounding spruce forest, a

*Sockeye salmon swim miles upstream to mate and die, subsequently surrendering their lives for that of a future generation. To capture this image without interfering with the salmon's natural mating behavior, I had to slide into the icy waters of a tributary that feeds the Russian River in Alaska and wait for the fish to pass by at a depth no greater than 12 inches.*W

soft silhouette appeared—a figure of an undistinguishable man old with time. His footsteps seemed ghostly as he moved so slowly and silently as not to break even a twig. There were no hints of the man's identity in the darkness, but as he entered the ring of light from the small glowing campfire, I recognized the man as the one who had left this place for a better one more than 30 seasons ago to complete the great circle of life.

It had been Laughing Eagle's voice that I recognized riding the wind; it was he who stood before me. The cast of firelight created a soft golden red glow that danced across the dead man's face. It revealed the same leathery skin and sparkling eyes I remembered. Eyes that still flickered with a magic of their own. It was an unaged, familiar face from the archives of my mind.

"My son, have you forgotten your past, the words of our elder, the tribal storyteller, the keeper of tribal traditions, he who was filled with the knowledge and wisdom of all who had gone before him? *Kuwatuhena elaihosihtit aesisak.* Animals are predictable. It is we humans who are the unpredictable ones.

"We have forgotten our past," sang the wind, or was it Laughing Eagle? "Animals are creative and smart. They use all their knowledge wisely and learn from their past. A mighty warrior and great teacher is the grizzly. He has the ability to destroy and eat of his choosing, yet he has chosen to avoid man whenever possible. He uses all of his knowledge to decide whether to bluff charge, attack, or flee. Unlike the grizzly, a brave will forget his knowledge and teachings. He may bolt like a deer, screaming, climb a tree like a squirrel, or fall to the earth and freeze like an opossum. He may even approach and strike like a rattler.

"Remember your past, my son. Where the water runs sweet, the animals drink.

Where the air is bright and clean, the animals flourish. Remember, the deep forest and seas; respect every wild creature and its homeland, for they have sustained and renewed our people for a thousand generations and will do so again if only given the chance. Live in harmony once again."

Off in the distance, I now could hear the murmuring voices and lost laughter of children, a chant among the willows and spruce, their spirit riding the open wind. Tears rolled down my cheeks—or was it the melting snowflakes that awakened me to the first snow of season in Denali National Park? Lying there, I reflected on feelings from my childhood of being thrilled and frightened at the same time. I shook as the smoldering fire cast wraiths into the new dawn's glow. Shivering, I snuggled deeper into my sleeping bag. "I'm tired; it must be the cold," I tried to convince myself. "Must be the cold."

Perhaps, I mused, it was the wisdom, insight, or whispering of the wind that helped Denali National Park create and enforce its unique policies and procedures. My first trip into the park, like that of all the other tens of thousands of visitors who journey north each year, was filled with anticipation and wonder even though I had special dispensation as a photographer/biologist and the much sought-after and highly limited private-vehicle photographer pass.

Park ranger Kevin Johnson booked me on the first bus into Denali that day. I arrived at Denali's main visitor center at 5 a.m. to meet my bus and fellow riders. I was dressed in my usual backcountry clothes, chosen for function, not fashion. My hiking boots were soft, comfortable, waterproof, and Gore-Tex lined. Based on the excess miles they had covered, their warranty would have expired if they were an automobile. My well-worn, loose-fitting, heavy-duty cotton pants were a camouflage brown; my thick-flannel, long-sleeve, duck-boat-green shirt was equally attractive. And my hat, well, let's say Indiana Jones would have been pleased. I wanted to be as unobtrusive and unnoticeable to the wildlife as possible.

I boarded the bus with my camera gear: four Leica camera bodies and a variety of Leica lenses. The lenses ranged from a 60 macro for creepy, crawly, flying insects

Denali's Buses Benefit All

The elimination of the use of personal vehicles and the use of buses instead at Denali National Park are beneficial to the ecosystem, wildlife and park visitors. Here are some of the benefits of this transformation plan:

- Reductions in fuel use lowers auto emissions, saves money and improves air quality.

- Decline in runoff of oil and antifreeze reduces impact on soil, water and vegetation.

- Reduction in number of vehicles means less noise and no traffic jams caused by animal sightings.

- Use of bus improves opportunities to spot animals from a higher vantage point across tundra and with 40 sets of eyes instead of one or two sets.

- Reduced opportunities for wildlife to be pursued or fed by visitors allows animals to remain independent for nourishment and makes viewing conditions more natural.

- Wild animals can do what they do naturally—eat, sleep and reproduce—and visitors get to see what they do naturally.

and the myriad of rainbow-colored wild-flowers to wide angles for vast panoramas and an 800mm for long-distance shots of caribou, moose, marmot, and grizzly bear.

Strapped to the side of my Sundog camera backpack was a Gitzo tripod with Wimberly floating head coupled to a quick-release mounting bracket. Fifty or so rolls of film joined my cameras and lenses inside the main pack. I hoped that would be enough to get me through the day. For snacks, I carried beef jerky in an airtight bag so as not to attract unwanted visitors; a can of tuna accompanied by packets of mayonnaise, several slices of bread, one can of soda, and a canteen of water. I also had some airtight bags to pack my garbage out.

In the sides and front pockets of my pack I always keep the same things: extra batteries in case a camera goes dead, and all too often one does; a lens cleaning cloth; Leica Trinovid 8 x 20 binoculars for spotting wildlife; the compass my wife gave me at Christmas, a reminder to find my way home; and a Swiss Army knife, the one with all the doodads. In my pack were a thermal shirt for changes in tempera-ture, which often occur at high altitudes; a pair of dry wool socks for wet feet; a rain poncho in case I got caught in a sudden downpour; a cigarette lighter for starting fires; and, of course, a space blanket for warmth—all the basic necessities for day trips into backcountry wilderness areas. I had more gear in my not-so-big backpack than everybody else on the bus combined and all of them had seen me in my last-minute arrival.

Jim, our driver, must be an early riser, because he was wide awake, bright-eyed and overflowing with good humor. "Good morning!" he boomed as I climbed aboard. "Arrgh" was all I could muster. An early morning school bus—boy did that bring back memories, especially since the only open seat was one over the wheel well.

Why were we taking a bus? It was the park's good fortune and that of its natural residents that the poor road system was impossible to upgrade to handle the influx of visitor vehicular traffic after the opening of the superhighway between Anchorage and Fairbanks.

People generally are not overly affec-tionate about Denali's policies. It is not

Most North American cat species are elusive and next to impossible to photograph in the wild. This Canadian lynx, like ninety-nine percent of all publishable lynx and mountain lion photos today, was taken under controlled conditions. C

When it comes to viewing and photographing wildlife such as this caribou, no amount of planning can replace good luck, but, it seems the more we know about an animal's habits and habitats, the luckier we get. W

because they are limited in activities or access. As a whole those limitations are no more restrictive than they are in other national parks. The displeasure has to do with America's love affair with their automobiles and their need to be in control.

We need to drive ourselves, stop where we want, and get out when we want. We think we need that control, and Denali takes some of it away. We can get out whenever and wherever we want except at a wildlife sighting or in a critical habitat. Park policy is such that no one can get off a bus within one-quarter mile of a sighting of most animals and one-half mile of bears and wolves.

Park and refuge policies that control where we walk and how many people may walk in a particular area benefit both visitors and the visited. Policies have to be created because most people cannot seem to control themselves or follow the rules without strict enforcement. Denali's policies do nothing more than force people to

become responsible for their actions and make their behavior more predictable. Predictability allows wildlife to know where, when, and what to expect from visitors. This design by accident created a prototype park that opened the eyes of park policy makers, wildlife biologists, conservationists and tourists throughout the world. These park policies, when followed and enforced, ultimately become a win-win situation for both man and beast.

Buses are one way of controlling people while still granting access to a great number of people. No one is allowed off a Denali bus within a designated distance of a wild creature, so there is no harassment of the animal through approach. Feeding wild animals, another American pastime, also is kept to a minimum, so animals do not become dependent on humans or look to them as a source of nutrients.

Today, the trend is to visit America the beautiful from sea to shining sea at speeds in excess of 55 miles per hour. An estimat-

These moose, like all wildlife species, are at home regardless of the weather

ed 95 percent of visitors to all national parks arrive by auto and spend seven times as much time inside as outside their vehicle; 16 percent never leave their vehicle, when the majority of people stop, it is to approach or feed a wild animal.

Park policy in Denali is similar to that in McNeil River State Game Sanctuary and Katmai National Park in Alaska. For a variety of reasons, each of them places the preservation of the environment and wildlife first and the enjoyment of the people second.

Within miles of the Denali visitor center and just as the sun crested the horizon, we came upon our first of many wildlife sightings, a bull moose, its antlers still in velvet. This grand and majestic creature was standing only feet from the roadside and bus. Like most moose in this area, he probably had spent his summer feeding on the aquatic vegetation of the tundra marshes and ponds. Now, this reclusive and solitary member of the deer family would spend the short autumn browsing on new growth and sprouts of mountain willows and other wetland plants. A good first sighting I thought and proving once again that early morning is one of the best times of day to see wildlife.

Excitement hummed among the visitors, and the bus tipped in the direction of the moose as everyone moved to one side for a better look. The moose was clad in thick, dark brown to black fur and had matching colored eyes, so it blended in with the thickly forested wetlands. The first indication of the upcoming rut or mating season was also evident with a touch of red blood permeating the chocolate-colored velvet on its eight-foot-wide antlers. Soon the moose would peel off the velvet by rubbing its magnificent antlers against small stands of willow and spruce. Autumn is the most aggressive time of year for the bulls. They protect and defend territory and cows at almost any cost. They become so aggressive they attack automobiles and even trains.

How funny we must have looked to the moose as we left the big, noisy, yellow bus and lined up on a single dirt path and pointed our cameras and binoculars at him!

About 15 minutes later, we continued our journey into the heart of Denali National Park. It was a splendid, crisp, clear morning as we rounded the mountain crest at mile marker 17, some 75 miles from the Mt. McKinley, and a hush fell over the bus. The silence quickly turned into small murmurs, then into a sea of excitement. "Mount McKinley!" There it stood, ominous by any stretch of the imagination, etched in stone and ice against an unblemished powder-blue sky. It was the first day that season that North America's tallest mountain was visible from such a great distance.

His story, his face and his expression were never so vivid in my mind as when I first looked upon the mountain—that mountaineer, whom by chance I had had dinner with several nights earlier. His name eludes me, but I will never forget his story, a story that took on an even greater impact when I saw Mt. McKinley. This was his mountain and his kind of day. This is his story:

"The long-term forecast sounded promising and the weather had finally broken. It looked like a good day to start our ascent of Mount McKinley, but, as mountains go, the weather is like a clock, always changing. The problem is, it changes without predictability, and Mount McKinley is definitely no exception.

"Our team had been waiting impatiently many weeks; I had been waiting a lifetime. Now it was time to fulfill our dreams. At first the trek was easy; gentle slopes with an occasional rough rock outcropping, but all in all easy. We had chosen the traditional route up the mountain; there was no sense in reinventing the wheel. But as we climbed higher, the rock faces grew increasingly steeper and more sheer. Sheets of ice covered large shaded sections of the slopes, and water dripped in sunny areas. Snowdrifts chest deep with hidden ice crevasses of unknown depth below our feet slowed our journey to a snail's pace. We faced treachery with each step.

"The days, weeks, months, and years I had trained, studied and prepared for this venture were finally paying off. Frost and ice capped my beard and mustache; my hands cramped with numbness from the cold and dampness; my body ached where it had never ached before and I reached deeper inside than I thought I could to conjure up more strength. There I found an innermost pain that hurt so good, a renewed strength, a grip to life.

"Everyone was exhausted and the summit was now only two and a half days away when, to our dismay, a snowstorm arose from out of nowhere. The granddaddy of them all. At higher elevations winds can easily reach speeds of 150 miles per hour, and this storm exceeded that. The blizzard with its pelting snow forced us to make camp—a godsend, for it gave us time to rest and recover even though the air was thin.

"For the next two days nobody moved, nobody left their tents. Each was isolated at, or at least near, the top of the world in single-man tents. Sleep quickly consumed and filled my body, encouraged by sore muscles and bones and nurtured by the lack of oxygen.

"Morning on the third day I was awakened out of a deep sleep by the noise of a deafening silence, a stillness seldom heard on any mountain or in any natural state. The storm had passed. I burrowed out of my tent and was temporarily blinded by the early morning light. Blinking, I savored the new day, grand and glorious by anyone's standards. Standing up I took a deep breath and filled my lungs with pure, clean, fresh air. No real signs of the passing storm were evident, with the exception of new snowdrifts and new open rock faces. The whirling winds conjured up by the passing storm had changed and transformed the mountain in many little ways, but nothing drastic. The sun was shining brightly just over the horizon. Thinking I was the first one out, I looked around only to find another member of what I believed was our climbing party sitting, facing the sunrise with a cup in his hand. An ominous aura strangely enveloped him; I didn't recognize his parka. He was meditating, contemplating the new day, or so I thought. I walked over to join him, touched his shoulder, and said 'good morning' in a church-like voice. He didn't acknowledge my greeting.

"His icy blue eyes were fixed on the beauty around him, and a peaceful, tranquil expression was on his lips. That's when I realized he wasn't part of our climbing expedition. He had been a member of an unsuccessful team that had gone out many years ago only to be consumed by the mountain. His icy grave had been uncovered by the whirling winds of the blizzard, but he would return to the depths with the next snowfall."

Snapping out of my trance-like state, not knowing if seconds or minutes had passed in the bus, I had a renewed appreciation of the mountain—and of the mountaineer.

Jim, our driver, was a slight, middle-aged man with silver gray hair. He was a wonderful narrator, offering naturalist facts and tales about each animal we came upon and those we hoped to see. He provided tidbits and information about the tundra, its plant life, even the pioneers and researchers, such as Adolf Murie, who first came to this magical land to study a world unimpeded by man. His anecdotes, his facts and fiction, were funny and sad. They tickled the fancy of everyone on the bus.

Sable Pass, mile marker 45: there it was bigger than life, the master of all North American land mammals and supreme in his realm, what everyone had traveled thousands of miles to see—a griz. A cinnamon colored grizzly bear was feeding on gooseberries, which provided nutrition for the bear's fatty buildup to carry it through the long months of hibernation.

Grizzlies are similar to us. They continue to learn throughout their lives, which last about 30 years in the wild. They are

Showing herself in full view only a few days a year, North America's highest mountain, Mount McKinley, rises above the glacial plain and tundra meadows of Denali National Park .

the news, and this mind-your-own-business grizzly feeding on gooseberries was not about to make the headlines. Someone up front asked Jim, "Why can't I get out? He's so cute, I am sure he wouldn't hurt me." Some folks jokingly call this "natural selection."

Our noisy yellow vehicle was obvious. Bears are very alert predators. With all our racket, could the bear be deaf or blind? With few exceptions, every bear I had ever encountered turned tail and ran when it sighted or scented me. Denali's grizzles have become habituated to humans. This grizzly did not even glance up, sniff the air or acknowledge our presence. To him, we were just another life form, neither to eat nor be eaten, and we offered him nothing he needed or feared.

I was like a kid in a candy shop. What an incredible opportunity, I thought, while loading another roll of film. (Usually it takes about 20 seconds to change a roll of film, but when I am in a hurry it takes at least 45.) We are so close to this grizzly I can use a standard portrait lens on my camera instead of a long telephoto lens. I could spend a lifetime in almost any other park or refuge and never get the quantity and quality of images I would capture at this one stop, but I would not know if I succeeded until I returned home and developed the pictures.

A variety of images of a grizzly bear doing what it does naturally, being a bear, was my prize. If I had been in a car I would not have seen this bear. Our vantage point from the bus had put us just above the tundra's dense vegetation.

A dozen or so miles up the road, my heart still racing from the grizzly bear sighting, I attempted to disembark from the bus for a hiking adventure on my own.

No getting off here, no exception! Sable Pass was closed to protect its critical habitat and no one could hike there. So, to

omnivorous, feeding primarily on vegetation, berries, roots and an occasional high-protein snack of insects or meat in the form of arctic ground squirrel or marmot. If the opportunity arises, grizzly bears may take down a caribou, moose, or sheep, usually the unhealthy, old or young ones. In spring they comb the valleys looking to feed on the thawing carcasses of the winter's kill. Denali's grizzlies are much smaller than their coastal cousins, who gorge themselves on spawning salmon all summer.

Over the clicking sound of camera shutters I could hear the excited chattering of fellow visitors: "It must be 800 to 1,000 pounds, you think?" "No. It must be at least 1,200, and I'll bet it stands 12 to 15 feet tall," responded another. A total misconception. Childhood tales and bad media hype have altered our perception of reality. This was an average size grizzly weighing about 400 pounds and standing maybe 8 feet tall. "Did you hear about the guy that got mauled over in..." Bears not lured into trouble by people almost never make

Some animal species were born to be eaten like this prolific arctic ground squirrel seen nibbling on a blade of grass. He is the second step in converting and transferring the sun's energy up the food chain for larger predators.

W

avoid accidentally venturing into a closed area, I waited until we were some distance away from the pass before disembarking. I hiked up a stone–laden stream for several hours. I walked away from any sign, sight, or sound of man, and I entered a glacier-sculpted land lost in time. A fragrant sweet smell hung in the air. I could almost taste the abundant cranberries, gooseberries, and blueberries.

Miles from the road the sounds of water grew more thunderous. A force great enough to create this expansive riverbed probably a half-mile across seemed inconceivable. The water's journey downstream is extremely turbulent during the annual spring thaw when the powerful currents tear through the riverbed bottom and embankments and displace boulders the size of cars.

With late-autumn approaching, this stream continued its more peaceful sojourn, a trickle of dust–laden water from the glacier above. Soon even this flow would be suspended in animation by winter's first freeze.

My detailed park topographical map and a compass reading gave me a clear route. I followed the connecting game trails through the intertwined tundra vegetation. I intended to intercept the park road at a point farther into the park.

At first glance the tundra landscape looked like a thickly piled rolling carpet, but this illusion quickly was shattered. The tundra's plant life varies in height and girth. It appears flat and level when viewed across the surface; the tops of the plants appear to be on the same plane. But the land hidden below the plants is rolling, dipping, and rising. At one point I stood ankle deep in a patch of thick cranberry and blueberry bushes overlooking the tundra. Then I took another four steps only to disappear into a head–high grove of nearly impassable 200-year-old willows whose 10- to 12-inch trunks and branches were twisted and bent.

In these depressions of the tundra nutrients and water gather and concentrate, providing nourishment for growing and sustaining large plants. The apparent flat and level-looking tundra is caused by winter winds that shear and prune the plants' tops and by winter-foraging wildlife that nip next year's buds at the snow line. Together, these forces never allow the plant growth to exceed the snow line created by centuries of harsh winter.

I chose the high ground and walked along the base of mountain ridges; below were large rocks and open gravel washes where shorter bushes and grasses predominated. By following this route rather than the streambed, walking was easier, and I could enjoy the more scenic view over the densely vegetated, glacially sculpted valleys below.

At the slightly higher elevations, a refreshing breeze gently blew and time passed quickly. Just over the next ridge I should be able to see the road. My hike

Interacting with Wildlife

Having a fascination with the large mammals that inhabit many of our national parks, I had always wanted to work in Denali. As a well-traveled visitor to many parks, I also thought I had seen it all.

What, after all, could be more impressive than watching and listening to a group of bull elk bugling on a crisp autumn morning in Yellowstone or seeing the last rays of the setting sun silhouette four large-antlered mule deer on a canyon rim in southern Utah? No less impressive is viewing the playful antics of black bear cubs in Yosemite or seeing bison challenge for dominance at Wind Cave. The mere presence of these magnificent animals provides us with a privileged snapshot of how our world once was.

Despite all my research and preparation, I still was unprepared for Denali. Though similarities were common, differences unfolded that clearly magnified my sense of awe. Denali does not portray how our wildlife once were, but rather how they still are.

Denali is the one traditional national park where the wildlife is truly wild, where man's influence has not yet altered the behavior of its inhabitants. But how long will that remain true? We now are experiencing the same kind of pressure long associated with our sister parks in the lower 48. The days of 30,000 visitors per year are gone forever, and the effects are mounting.

Recognizing the potential impact on unlimited vehicle travel on wildlife near the Denali Park Road, national park managers made some difficult and far-reaching decisions. The 1972 private vehicle restrictions pried visitors out of their cars and onto the public bus system, thus drastically reducing the number of vehicles on the road.

The success of this system can be measured by the number and variety of animals viewed each day in their near natural state. Firsthand views of exceptional wildlife

interactions are not unusual. Caribou/wolf and bear/moose predation along with bear/wolf kill site interactions are seen annually by thousands of visitors.

Besides restricting private vehicles, a second and equally important step was taken by developing a Code of Ethics for the many photographers, photo–journalists and visitors who flock to view animals or capture them on film. This code, although sometimes maligned, sets forth guidelines for interacting with wildlife. Its overriding theme is simple and direct:"The welfare of the subject is more important than the photograph."

That thought is reinforced continually through interpretive programs, park publications and personal field contacts. Despite all our efforts, Denali wildlife still is pursued, annoyed, baited and harassed by visitors. Whether by ignorance or intent, such behavior unacceptable.

Animals that become aggressive or overhabituated are often described as exhibiting unacceptable behavior. Sadly, through no fault of their own, these animals must be destroyed. The irony is that our own unacceptable behavior is likely the cause.

Conservation unit managers and visitors alike, regardless of where they are located, must seriously assume the role they play in protecting our wildlife resources. Realistic measures such as Denali's Code of Ethics must be adopted. Creative ways to manage visitors while still providing them quality experiences need to be developed. Our wildlife is too cherished to put forth anything but our absolute best effort.

The ultimate responsibility for success or failure rests on all our shoulders.

Ken Kehrer, Jr.
Chief Ranger
Denali National Park

had been a good one, with bountiful wildlife sightings. I was able to stop, observe, and photograph numerous arctic ground squirrels, a hoary marmot, and a golden eagle gliding the thermals. I had chosen this particular route because it provided the least habitat impact and minimal wildlife disturbance. I also chose my path because it allowed me to observe the wildlife below from a greater perspective. Since leaving the bus, I walked with my 800mm lens mounted to my camera and tripod slung over my shoulder, ready to capture a picture at any moment. Thus far, I had exposed two rolls.

The road did not appear over the next ridge, but, better yet, a small herd of grazing caribou appeared off in the valley below. I had never seen a "bou," the local name for caribou, in the wild before, but I knew about the behavior of other members of the deer family. I knew how to traverse dense thickets and what course a wild creature might choose. Now it was time to put my years of experience to work and get close enough for some good pictures without disturbing my subjects, seven bulls with magnificent racks, the tallest antlers I had ever seen. Each rack had to be at least six feet in height.

It is hard to believe these animals gather in herds by the tens of thousands to migrate between wintering and calving grounds. Like a massive river, they travel over snow–covered tundra, swim icy lakes and forge raging rivers in search of greener pastures hundreds of miles away. Upon arrival the herd disperses and single members and small bands forage and wander an additional thousand or more miles.

From where I had first spotted the "bous" I watched for some time to determine their normal behavior, uninhibited by people or predators. I watched how often each member raised its head between bites of vegetation. Did they look around; did they sniff the air for predators; did they lay down; how fast did they move, and in what direction? I observed from a distance with binoculars and gathered all the information I needed to properly set up and photograph the caribou without disturbing them.

I looked at the sun's passage to take advantage of its lighting in my photography. I checked to see which way the wind was blowing so as to keep my scent blowing away from my subjects. Through my observations and knowledge of animal behavior, and by studying the lay of the land, I determined the direction the caribou were moving, so I could intercept their course without disrupting them. Before moving, I tried to estimate the time it would take me to reach that point.

I moved very slowly and quietly. The small herd also moved toward that same point but a little slower then I estimated, partly because of the heat. These creatures are designed for cold weather, and that day was warm. Their coats contain hollow air-filled guard hairs designed to create good winter insulation and greater buoyancy for crossing water during their annual migrations.

There is no place for impatience in wildlife photography, because animals have no schedules or appointments to keep. So I sat patiently for them to approach. In knowing that park animals are more complacent than those in hunted populations, I purposely chose a place to sit that was somewhat exposed to their view. I did that in case they sensed my presence and so I would not be confused with or considered a potential predator but only a tourist. As anticipated, they slowly walked up the glacial valley only a few yards in front of me on their widespread hooves, evolved for crossing soft marshes and snow–covered tundra. When they finally realized I was there, because of my camera noise, they stopped and looked at me. Then, realizing I posed no threat, they continued on their way. After they were a good distance away, I proceeded on my way, stumbling to the road over the ridge to intercept the next bus.

In Denali, the animals have more or less become accustomed to humans. Park policies have allowed people to become predictable. As a result, animals live uninhibited by visitors and visitors see more wildlife.

Only after the release of my first frame of film did this caribou know of my presence. Allowing an animal to come to you can often yield much better viewing opportunities and photographic results than those achieved through following and stalking an animal.

Backcountry Trailing

"Alaska is different," they say. Certainly Denali National Park is unlike most old, well-established national parks in the lower 48. Here visitors must leave their cars behind and access the park on shuttle buses or on foot. Marked, maintained trails exist in only a tiny fraction of its six million acres, but still thousands of people hike into the Denali wilderness every year.

I first experienced hiking in Denali many years ago as a visitor. I was an experienced backpacker, having logged many miles on trails all over the lower 48. Denali, then called Mt. McKinley National Park, was indeed different! There were no trails, no bridges, no signs, and no markers, just big, wide-braided river valleys and long ridges beckoning one to explore a vast expanse of wilderness on the flanks of the massive, snow-mantled Alaska Range.

After diligently studying our topographic maps to plan our route, my companion and I spent several days pushing our way through tangles of dwarf birch and willow, making numerous bone-chilling stream crossings, and gingerly hopping our way across bogs on treacherous, ankle-twisting tussock. Gravelly river bars provided easier passage, for both us and wildlife, as numerous grizzly bear, wolf, caribou, and moose tracks attested. And walking the high ridges and passes on a soft carpet of tundra bright with fall colors was a joy. We crossed paths with caribou, Dall sheep, grizzly bear, and ptarmigan. Signs of wildlife were everywhere, but there were no traces of other people.

Intimidating? A bit. Rewarding? Yes! Trails certainly would have eased our travel. But the remarkable abundance of wildlife we encountered and the sense of solitude and self-reliance we felt would have been missing. These challenges and rewards are still available today for anyone willing to venture cross-country into Denali's wilderness, whether on a day hike or a multi-day trip.

Denali's remarkable wilderness character has survived in the face of growing visitation, in large part because of a policy in effect since 1973 and formalized in the 1984 Backcountry Use Plan. This policy, according to the park's General Management Plan, is to "provide backcountry opportunities for visitors while preventing vegetation damage..., the creation of trails and campsites, and other signs of human use which compromise wilderness values, and minimizing human impacts upon wildlife." The designated wilderness area is managed under a "no marked, maintained trails" policy and is zoned into backcountry units with limited overnight permits issued for each, so no area is overused.

Even with this policy and plan, trails can just happen with the passage of many pairs of hiking boots along popular routes. To prevent this from occurring, park rangers thoroughly brief wilderness users on minimum impact hiking and camping techniques prior to issuing backcountry use permits. For example, hikers are encouraged to choose routes along river bars, which can withstand use. Groups are instructed to spread out as they walk to disperse their impact rather than walking single file and creating "social trails."

Much of the success or failure of this effort lies with individuals and the decisions they make about ethical behavior while in the backcountry. It will take continuation of this strong partnership between park staff and park visitors to assure that the vision of a trail-less Denali wilderness remains a reality.

Thea Nordling
Chief of Interpretation
Denali National Park

*The best places to observe and photograph wildlife are in national parks, national wildlife refuges and national forests. In here wildlife generally considers humans as bothersome nuisances, not as predators.*W

Part Two: General Advice

Where to Start Finding Wildlife

"Nature cannot be ordered about, except by obeying her."
—Francis Bacon

To observe and photograph wild animals, we first must find them. Sometimes that is simple, but more often than not it is difficult. The more we know about wild animals—what they look like, where they live, their needs, their behavior patterns—the more likely we will find the creatures we seek.

It is fun to approach the problem of finding wildlife like a naturalist's version of the game of Jeopardy. All the answers are there. We just have to recognize them. The more we know about an animal and follow specific wildlife signs, the more likely we are to solve the puzzle and find the subject. This approach is most rewarding when we are attempting to find the more elusive mammals, but no matter how well we put the pieces together, we still might get only a fleeting glance of certain species.

Naturalist skills develop with education, practice, patience, and time. Unfortunately, many people today have fewer opportunities to learn about nature firsthand. As a youngster, when time seemed to last forever, I spent countless hours exploring in the woods by myself or with my father, woodsmen, hunters, Native Americans and other friends who more or less depended on the natural world for their subsistence. They taught me what type of habitat supports what animals, when and where animals breed, when they migrate. They showed me how to identify animal tracks, droppings and hair follicles. In time, and with a lot of practice, I was able to identify a wild creature and find where it lived without seeing it.

For every animal we see, ten or more have already seen us and have moved off into hiding.

Today, for most of us, time is a costly and diminishing commodity. We cannot afford weeks or months, never mind a year, in the field studying animals and their habitats. However, there are some good alternative ways to learn about nature: publications, journals, television shows, videos and interactive computer programs. We can learn the basics about any subject at any time from the comfort of our homes.

If you are beginning a quest to follow your dreams of seeing and photographing scenic areas, plants, and wildlife, hook up with others who have similar dreams. Join nature, outing, hiking, birding, camera, diving, fishing and hunting organizations. Join your local chapters of the Audubon Society, Sierra Club, Wildlife Conservation Society, National Wildlife Federation and other groups. Each organization offers different opportunities to learn from people who have the same interests and often a great deal of knowledge about natural history.

Visit zoos, aquariums, museums, and wildlife rehabilitation centers. They are great for learning about where animals live, population dynamics, behavioral patterns, mating habits and migrations. When visiting, take time to read interpretive exhibit signs, which usually contain a great amount of information.

The best places to find wildlife are our national parks, national wildlife refuges and national forests. These places were set aside to protect their abundant wildlife and to preserve habitats. In parks and refuges, wildlife is generally safe from people and therefore considers humans bothersome nuisances but not predators. Resident wildlife is more tolerant and accustomed to people than migrant species.

When arriving at a park, even if you have been there many times, stop at the gate, visitor center, or park office to ask the naturalist or ranger what educational programs are being offered that day. Ask if there have been any recent interesting species sightings and find out where. This information might lead to a good starting point for your visit.

While in a park or refuge, look for fellow photographers and wildlife observers. If they have stopped to set up their cameras, spotting scopes or binoculars, chances are good they have seen something. Quietly pull off the road where it is legal to do so. Turn off your radio, close your vehicle doors and trunk lid as quietly as possible and follow the basic rules of protocol for photographers and viewers. Do not be afraid to ask questions of others, especially if they look like they might know what they are doing. That is a good way to learn.

When looking for a place to find wildlife and wildlife information, do not overlook

The white spots of the fawn allow it to blend in naturally with its surroundings. If you are fortunate to come upon a young animal never touch it— your scent may cause the mother to abandon it. C

the obvious. Start close to home at local, county and state parks. They are wonderful places to learn the basics about nature and that will help you when you go on that dream vacation to one of our national parks, national wildlife refuges, or national forests. Also, these local parks are good places to test new pieces of camera equipment, for you can easily return them and try something different.

Community colleges and universities offer a variety of programs and courses for both adults and children. Workshops are another good way to learn more about photography equipment and how to use it. Fishing and hunting clubs often offer programs about the environment and wildlife. Public libraries have many reference books and magazines that provide current information about natural history.

For a wonderful hands-on experience, volunteer in a park, wildlife refuge or other natural area. Most of them are short-handed and

can use a pair of helping hands. At many of them volunteers have become a valuable resource. A few hours each month can be extremely rewarding.

The more you know about wildlife, the more success you will have in finding and photographing your sought-after subjects and fulfilling your dreams. The better you become at finding wildlife, the less disruptive you will be and the more likely you will fulfill your dreams.

Study the animals. Observe their movements, sounds and calls. Walk nature trails, because most wild animals found along them have grown accustomed somewhat to people and thus are easier to see than those in the wilderness.

Whenever I visit natural areas, I try to take someone with me to share the experience. If I can, I take someone who is more knowledgeable, so I learn. And I try to be as curious as a youngster.

Photographer/Viewer Protocol

If you plan to photograph wildlife and other natural features, here are some guidelines to follow whether you are an amateur or a professional:

- Respect wildlife and its habitat.

- Make sure your activity does not interfere or infringe upon someone else's wildlife experience.

- If an individual is photographing or viewing specific animals that you are interested in, ask politely if you may join.

- Do not walk in front of other viewers and photographers.

- Do not block trails, roadways or dominant overlooks.

- Become familiar with and follow the managing agency's rules and regulations.

- Never enter any area that is not open to the public and never engage in prohibited activities.

Where Are the Animals?

More than nine million visits annually makes Great Smoky Mountains National Park the most visited unit in the National Park System. One of the most common questions asked by visitors upon arrival after "Where are the bathrooms?" is "Where are the bears?" or "Where can I see wildlife?"

Within its 800 square miles of mountains, the park is a haven for wildlife and is well known for its diversity. Black bears are fairly commonly seen during the summer when berries are ripe and young males seek out mates. White-tailed deer are abundant and easily viewed in areas such as Cades Cove or Cataloochee.

The number of other mammal species exceeds 60. Some are commonly seen, such as raccoon, groundhog, and skunk. More reclusive mammals that reward the frequent and careful observer could include mink, bobcat, river otter, or coyote. Besides mammals, the Smokies boasts great diversity in birds, insects, reptiles, amphibians, flora, and landscapes.

The diversity of visitors is perhaps as great as the wildlife species. They range from backpackers to those who never exit their vehicle, from anglers to picnickers, from nature photographers to home video enthusiasts, from day hikers to campers. All welcome the opportunity to view wildlife, but each approaches the activity with different levels of experience and common sense.

Is wildlife affected by viewers and vice versa? Yes. Are the activities of preserving species and desiring to observe them compatible? They can be, if people recognize they are the visitors within a natural system and treat it with respect. When the line is crossed between being courteous visitors and being intruders, interactions can become detrimental and, at times, dangerous. A park visitor should not approach close enough to change an animal's behavior. Different species and individuals have a different flight distance, the imaginary circle that reflects the closest distance an animal will tolerate a predator or perceived threat before fleeing or defending itself. What about black bears? One cannot say that approaching no closer than 400 feet of a bear is safe.

Common sense needs to be the rule of thumb. When wildlife becomes habituated to close human interaction, it is at greater risk. If observation causes the animal to move on, make eye contact, or in any way change behavior, one should assume the line has been crossed and back off. One should remember to be cautious rather than risk affecting an animal's behavior. Telephoto lenses, binoculars, and keen eyes can allow one to enjoy viewing wildlife involved in its natural habits.

Feeding an animal may seem to do little harm, but in reality it often shortens the animal's life, because behavior changes may bring the animal in close contact with people, roads, and vehicles.

Ultimately, when people and wildlife interact, it is the wildlife that suffers.

Karen Wade
Superintendent
Great Smoky Mountains National Park

Workshops and Tours

The growth and interest in workshops and tours about photography and the environment have been phenomenal. In recent years new tour companies and workshops have sprung up all across the country. Their appeal is widespread, for most of us would rather avoid the aggravation of stumbling around on our own and invest in someone else's experience to improve our opportunities to see and photograph spectacular wildlife and beautiful scenic locations.

This growth has occurred with the spawning of a new awareness about the environment and the preservation of our Earth and all species that live here. Large public interest groups have replaced the individual efforts of people like John Muir. Now, both teacher and student are expected to exhibit a high level of care and caution when in the field.

This change in thinking can be seen in the remarks of a comedian who years ago said he would always remember these words of wisdom: "Always carry a trash bag in your car, and when its full, just toss it out the window." No doubt he was joking, but he probably would rather slither under rocks than make a statement like that today.

As an instructor and tour leader, I believe workshops and tours have an obligation to convey a high degree of concern for our environment from simple things like recycling our trash on our trips to educating groups about fragile environments we may encounter along the way.

You can learn a lot about loving nature properly from experienced workshop and tour leaders.

Gary W. Stanley
Professional Photographer/Tour Leader

Giving Back to Nature

Nature study, bird-watching, and nature photography are among the favorite out-door activities of Americans. According to surveys, tens of millions of us enjoy these pursuits, far more than hunt or fish or pan for gold. Everyone, not just a small elite, gets huge benefits from open lands, parks, wilderness, and the wildlife that inhabits them. From clean air, water, and food for daily existence to natural scenes that soothe the soul, gifts of nature enrich us all. Every aspect of nature is worthy of respect and holds a place of honor on Earth.

Despite this, natural areas and nature in general are under constant and growing attack from the other side of human behavior--our industrial, product-oriented, convenience-loving, transport-mad, money-hungry, constantly-reproducing, con-sumer world. We are losing our balance. Now is not the time to lose our voice.

Nature lovers and photographers can be a powerful force. We should take every possible opportunity and we should make opportunities to teach about nature and encourage more knowledge and protection of our common environment. In 20 years of nature photography and environmental work, I have developed a list of goals for using my photographs. Like all good goals, they are lofty. Perfection and constant achievement are out of reach, but I try. Everything I photograph and love and rely on depends on these goals:

- Tell the truth—Get the whole story, including the threats and the destruction. Caption and explain accurately and completely. Try to learn the deeper meanings and background.

- Educate—Illuminate the world for all, especially children, leaders, and influen-tial, powerful people.

- Contribute—Volunteer your knowledge, pictures, time, money, and influence to groups involved in protecting nature.

- Be true to yourself, to your heart, and to nature—This is most difficult of the goals. It involves actually doing these things despite setbacks and daily living. It means thinking broadly and deeply but acting in ways you and others can grasp. And one must try to be honest and truthful when challenged, threatened, or asked to con-tribute to those who may be responsible for endangering the nature you love.

Gary Braasch
Professional Photographer/Freelance Writer

A closed area. Only through the protection of critical habitats can some species survive. C

Viewing and Photographing Techniques

"Man is everywhere a disturbing agent. Wherever he plants his foot the harmonies of nature are turned to discords."
—George Perkins Marsh

Finding wildlife is only one part of the process of viewing and photographing it. The other more important part is the manner in which we attempt to approach our subject. The issues surrounding our interaction with wildlife sometimes can be complicated and emotional because we naturally want to get as close as possible to wildlife even when we know otherwise.

We all can agree that most viewers and photographers of wildlife care a great deal about the creatures they wish to see, but too often our desires overshadow what is right and what is wrong. We may end up encroaching upon their space and potentially endangering ourselves and the wildlife. We may cause the creatures to stop feeding, interrupt a mating ritual, leave their young even temporarily, run off into hiding or attack us.

Those who cause the greatest disturbance to wildlife are often people toting cameras, followed closely by families with young children or, worse, an unleashed dog or domestic cat. Our sincere concerns and appreciation for nature do not diminish adverse effects on animals and habitats.

To reduce negative impacts, we need not avoid approaching animals altogether. Rather, we need to limit and modify our behavior, so we are less intrusive. We need to create a consistency that allows wildlife to become accustomed to more predictable human behavior.

Man's influence on wildlife behavior

Interpreting physical wildlife signs and understanding animal behavior often are easier in parks and refuges, where wild creatures are protected and where human activities are somewhat controlled, than in unrestricted areas where people can do pretty much as they please. The more con-

Late summer and autumn are good times to observe and photograph wildlife because many species are actively storing food for the coming winter. W

sistent we are as a species, the greater our chances of finding and seeing wildlife.

When we venture into a park or refuge, we usually see wildlife whose behavior has changed because it has become used to people. Other animals have moved off into the backcountry or into hiding. We can go to almost any of our national parks and national wildlife refuges and see wildlife. We can view elk and bison in Yellowstone National Park, Dall sheep and caribou in Denali National Park, wading birds in J.N. "Ding" Darling National Wildlife Refuge, moose and swans in Grand Teton National Park, elk on the National Elk Refuge, mountain goats and mule deer in Glacier National Park, bison on the National Bison Range, pronghorn antelope and prairie dogs in Badlands National Park, elephant seals and gannets in Channel Islands National Park, waterfowl in Brigantine National Wildlife Refuge, alligators and egrets in Everglades National Park and harbor seals and puffins in Acadia National Park. In all of them, most animals do not flee or hide like most wild animals.

Resident wildlife in many parks and refuges of the lower 48 states and in the southern provinces of Canada have modified their behavior because of environmental and human pressures. With all environmental factors being equal, it is often our direct interactions with wildlife that influence and determine if wildlife will survive and be viewed in a specific area. The greater the incidental and direct human pressure on an animal, the more its behavior patterns change.

Without thinking of the effects of our actions, we often approach wildlife much closer than we should. We unknowingly force wildlife to be on the move and unnecessarily burn up stored calories needed for survival. When we force an animal to run, it consumes strength and energy and may become tired and an easier target for predators. Tired animals may not have the strength necessary to survive winter, perform their mating rituals, gather enough food to feed their young and

other activities. Energy reserves are critical to survival during gestation, migration and hibernation. Interfere significantly and animals perish.

Approaching wildlife too closely can disrupt normal foraging patterns, and behavior changes can cause an increase or decrease in predation between species as well as normal relationships within a species.

If an animal is fed by people, it learns to depend on them for its food. If an animal is sought and chased after for photographs or hunted, survival instincts make it more elusive and skittish. Our inconsistent actions generate the greatest shift in species behavior. If all visitors walk only along designated trails within a given area, the resident wildlife can define perimeters and utilize the adjacent habitat up to the trail's edge. When we leave defined paths and go where we please, resident wildlife knows no boundaries and, like us, feels threatened by the unknown. We may be perceived as predators. Wildlife does not understand we only want to get a little closer to have a better look.

Being in the right area at the right time is only part of the solution in finding wildlife. The other is understanding wildlife behavior. Sometimes you have to be as agile as your subject in order to be successful. W

What to wear

We do not always think about it, but what we wear when we visit wilderness areas is as important as what we wear to a business meeting or a social event. Our clothing makes a statement, and sometimes we wear specific clothes for specific occasions. In natural areas, wear clothing that blends in with the environment.

● **Wear natural–colored clothing** such as deep greens, dark browns, and camouflage. If you are in the desert, wear sand and rust colors to match the surroundings. In a deep forest, wear dark greens and browns. Blend in with the season. If there is snow on the ground, wear white. Current leisure and sports clothing styles are bright and flashy. They look great, but when we wear these colors in natural areas, we stand out and advertise our presence to wildlife. Note: Wear bright-colored clothes during hunting seasons for safety, but do not anticipate seeing much wildlife while hunting is permitted.

● **Wear soft flexible clothing** of cotton or wool. Some of the newer composite fabrics also are good, but some synthetic materials and plastics can create loud scratching noises whenever you rub past a branch or twig.

● **Wear hiking boots or sneakers.** Their soles grip surfaces and help to keep us from slipping. Break in new boots prior to long hikes.

Flight Distances

All creatures, including humans, have a specific distance around them that is defined as personal space. This space belongs to that being and is not to be entered into without a reaction. For a wild animal, this distance often is referred to as its flight distance. When its flight distance is invaded or threatened, the animal, fearing for its life or that of its young, will flee. It also may assume a posture to protect itself based solely on its instinctive behavior and perception. The closer we get to wildlife, the more stressed the animal becomes. A sudden encroachment on an animal's flight distance may cause an instinctive reaction, and the animal may attack rather than flee.

The flight distance varies from species to species and individual to individual, but it usually is based upon size, strength, speed and gender. The time of year, the amount of pressure that man applies and the number of predators also affect a species' flight distance.

As mentioned earlier, animals exposed to a lot of positive interactions with people are more tolerant of us than those that have not been exposed. An animal that has been harassed by people will be less tolerant than ones that have not been harassed. An animal with young is less tolerant than others.

Approaching policies

An increasing number of parks and refuges are implementing and enforcing regulations pertaining to how and when visitors approach wildlife. Most national parks, national wildlife refuges and national recreation areas have such regulations, and the ever–increasing number of visitors makes it paramount that all of them adhere to regulations.

To help protect wildlife, check at visitor centers, ranger stations, and interactive exhibits for updated wildlife viewing information and regulations prior to venturing into remote areas. Each agency has its own set of policies, rules and regulations governing interaction with wildlife, and sometimes policies differ within an agency because of certain mandates.

Federal and state endangered or threatened species regulations get the highest priority in resource protection. Presently, the threatened and endangered species list consists of more than 900 species, and there are more than 3,700 additional potential candidates.

It is important to note that a prescribed approaching distance is the distance you may approach relative to an animal, not the distance an animal may travel in pursuing you. If you are sitting or standing in a specific spot and an animal decides to walk up to you, this is not considered "approaching." However, the impact on the wildlife is the same, and visitors should back off. If at all possible, always keep your distance with respect to wildlife and never entice a wild creature to approach you.

If you are unable to find out the closest distance and where you can legally approach wildlife, or if you are in doubt, use common sense and maintain a safe distance.

Check to see if the specific area you wish to visit in a park or refuge is open or is closed as a critical habitat. Some areas are closed seasonally to allow wildlife to successfully breed and raise their young. Some areas are temporarily closed because of natural events such as forest fires or wolf or grizzly bear kills.

An animal's behavior is usually altered when it is approached. This red-winged blackbird will leave its nest and attack visitors who wander too close W

Before approaching an animal, ask yourself if a glimpse or a photo is worth the effects generated by your approach.

When approaching

Animals utilize their senses of hearing, sight and smell to detect predators, including humans. A wild animal's senses are much more sophisticated and developed than that of humans. It is sometimes impossible for us to comprehend an animal's extraordinary natural abilities. A male silk worm moth, for instance, can detect a mate from a mile away. A hawk, eagle or falcon can spot a mouse in a field of grass from more than a 100 feet in the air. An owl, with its incredible hearing, can pinpoint its prey at night from 100 feet away based solely on the sound of rustling leaves or a chirp. A lizard can detect the slightest movement. A fox or wolf can smell a person from more than a half mile away. A deer can pick out the snapping of a twig by a foot from 100 feet. A mountain goat or sheep knows you are climbing a mountain before you ever see the animal.

Many people claim, although it has never been scientifically proven, that animals have a sixth sense, an uncanny ability to know something is not right or is present without relying on any of its five basic senses. Wild animals more often than not will detect our presence long before we see them—unless we outsmart them.

While in a park or refuge, never stalk an animal. True stalking in protected areas often results in chasing an animal away instead of getting a better look or photograph. Also, it is illegal to harass animals in a parks and refuges by chase or pursuit. In areas where hunting is permitted, however, stalking is one way you can get close enough to see and photograph wildlife.

Animals are skittish by nature.

If you plan to successfully view and photograph wildlife, never press them. Try to be as quiet as possible, for any slight irregular noise, smell or movement may cause them to flee into hiding.

Sometimes it is best to be alone while photographing nature and wildlife. At other times, small groups of people are appropriate, but large groups alter natural behavior and lead to fewer animal sightings.

When visiting a park or refuge, leave your pets at home. If you have your pets with you, always keep them leashed. Pets sometimes draw the attention of wild animals and may send them into hiding. You significantly reduce your chances of seeing wildlife by bringing your dog. When you exercise your pet, consider others and do not reduce their chances of seeing wildlife.

When stopping your vehicle to view wildlife, make sure the radio is off. If you get out, take the keys out of the ignition. The chiming of a car's warning system alerts wildlife—and you do not want to lock yourself out of your car in the middle of a remote area! After stepping out of your car, shut the door softly. Many people point at the wildlife to show the location to others; that often makes the animals nervous.

Move slowly even though it is exciting to see wildlife. Avoid sudden moves or loud noises that could startle an animal and send it into hiding. Move when the animal is feeding or distracted. Avoid walking when an animal is looking directly and intently at you; instead, wait for it to resume feeding.

By moving slowly and quietly, you allow wildlife to become accustomed to you and let them understand you mean no harm. When approaching an animal in a park or refuge, sometimes you can allow them to see you because they feel safe in the area. Never walk directly toward an animal; although predators are sneaky, they approach directly. Avoid making direct eye contact for it can be misconstrued as a challenge. Instead, look at other points of interest and where the animal is looking. If it looks at you, turn and look behind you as if there is something of greater importance—or threatening—beyond you.

If you are near or among browsing mammals, duplicate their meandering. As they zig and zag, mimic their behavior as much as possible and with each step work your way closer. Stop and look around occasionally. Bend and pick a blade or two of grass. Try to determine their direction and head toward a point of intersection, where you can wait for their approach.

Am I too close?

When we become familiar with wildlife behavior and how animals communicate through both their nervous and warning signs, we can better interact with them and anticipate what effects we have on their behavior. A common misperception is that if an animal raises its head, looks toward you or moves away, you are too close. You very well could be, but that is not always the case.

As a novice naturalist or one with little background knowledge in animal behavior, view wild animals from a distance with good binoculars, a spotting scope or a long telephoto camera lens. For example, observe how often an elk, caribou or ground squirrel moves and how often it raises its head and looks around. Based on these observations, determine its normal behavioral patterns and cycles. Try to observe an animal's natural behavior with no predator or perceived human-predators around, so you can properly determine if your approach is affecting its behavior.

To survive, an animal must always be on its guard. When observing browsing and grazing animals, notice they are always moving. They take a nip here and a bite there, then they move along. They always stop between bites to look up, smell the air and listen. If no danger is evident, they take another bite, stop, lift their head and look around, smelling and listening for potential trouble. Their survival instincts are at work.

The more predators a species has, the more nervous and fidgety the animals are and the more often they move and stop, look, listen and smell the air. Ground squirrels, marmots and other small species typically have limited home ranges and stay in close proximity of their dens in case they need a quick escape. They also are more skittish than larger species. They jump at the wind and scurry to their dens. If all is quiet, they soon emerge to forage again.

All animals move, stop, look, listen and sniff in a given and repeating pattern. An animal that exhibits any quick movements, stops feeding altogether, jumps, gets up quickly from resting, suddenly begins to swing its head, freezes or moves directly away has noticed something. These are basic nervous signals.

If you begin to approach an animal and it exhibits any of these signs, you are too close and are perceived as a predator. Slowly back off so you are no longer encroaching on its personal space. The distance you need to retreat is often much greater than if you would have kept a proper distance in the first place. If you are in doubt, do not approach. Use binoculars, a spotting scope or a long telephoto lens to enjoy your subject.

Nervous signs

Every animal can sense when it is being approached, and an animal usually senses our presence long before we realize it.

Look for behavioral signals that communicate it has sensed your presence, and look for warning signs of stress. You can save yourself a lot of trouble, perhaps even your life, if you can anticipate what an animal is going to do next. An animal's awareness, nervousness and warning signs are communicated by signals. Each signal occurs in a progression and increases steadily in intensity to a point at which an animal will accept the situation, flee or attack.

A classic example of an animal forecasting its intentions is when you meet a strange dog. The dog may wag its tail to show acceptance, tuck its tail between its legs to show submission or lower its tail and raise the hair on the back of its neck to warn you. If you continue to approach, the dog might curl its upper lip, expose its teeth, growl, and attack.

Wild animals are no different. They display similar warning signs in similar suc-

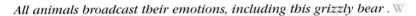

All animals broadcast their emotions, including this grizzly bear . W

cession, though there are exceptions, because each animal is an individual. If it is surprised or feels threatened or endangered, it may attack without warning.

Here are some examples of wildlife behavior signs:

● American bison

Most bison are not afraid of and do not care much about people. But when they are upset, they will stop what they are doing, glare, arch their backs, roll back their eyes and charge. More people are injured and gored each year by bison in our national parks than perhaps by any other animal. People spot bison grazing along roadsides and in meadows. Bison do not run when we get out of our cars and approach, so we see how close we can get, forgetting a bison is a very large powerful animal. They are not just another kind of cow, but a surprisingly fast and agile wild animal.

● Bears

At first a bear will extend its head out and up, sniffing the air to pick up scent. Then it may stand erect on its hind legs to get a better look at who or what is distracting it. If it is nervous or angry, the hair on its back will stand erect. It will pull back its ears before charging.

● Canines (wolf, fox)

These species freeze, lower and extend their head, smell the air, then look from side to side while still smelling to pinpoint their subject. When they are nervous, these canines forecast their emotions like domestic dogs: hair rising on the back of their necks, curling of upper lip and growling.

● Felines (cougar, bobcat, lynx)

These species—like domestic cats— will freeze in their tracks and slowly look around. When they are nervous, they twitch their tail and crouch down with their leg muscles tight, ready to flee.

● Rabbits and hares

These prey species freeze when being approached. They tense up their back leg muscles, ready for escape.

● Raptors

Birds of prey freeze, moving only their heads and utilizing their keen senses of hearing and sight to try to pinpoint whatever it is that is making them nervous.

● Rodents (beaver, squirrel, woodchuck, marmot, chipmunk, porcupine, skunk)

These species stand erect and freeze all movement. They extend their heads to look, listen, and sniff the air when they perceive something is approaching, but they take few chances and seldom linger. They are quick to run off into hiding.

● Ungulates (deer, moose, elk, caribou, antelope)

When first approached, they freeze with their head held high and their ears turned toward the approaching sound. They look and smell the air for signs of danger. A flick of their tails or a twitch of their ears signifies nervousness. The thumping of a front hoof on the ground or snorting is often an alarm to other ungulates. When their body hair stands erect and they flatten back their ears, they are about to charge.

● Waterfowl

When nervous, waterfowl crane or stretch their necks out and up as they look for threats and prepare for flight.

Animal curiosity

Countless wild creatures approach people strictly out of curiosity. It seems the farther away from civilization, roadsides and other people we go, the more likely we are to have such encounters. Sometimes in areas where animals are not hunted, they are curious about people.

If an animal shows curiosity, do not attempt to approach. Instead, sit and wait and look around, but never directly look at the approaching animal. Without paying direct attention to your subject, casually glance up at the approaching animal. If you need to stand, do so slowly, so your size does not frighten it.

While waiting, set up your camera equipment. Adjust the focus and exposure

All animals are curious by nature and fear is a learned behavior.Animals who do not fear man have either become habituated to them or have not been exposed to people. Remote areas of parks and refuges offer the best viewing and photographic opportunities W

as the animal approaches and take insurance shots just in case it gets nervous and backs off. Sometimes a curious animal may approach to within a few feet. Note: You still must be on the alert that the animal might charge you suddenly.

Alternatives to approaching

It is not always necessary or wise to approach wildlife, especially with species known to be skittish and elusive. In these situations, enjoy the animals from a distance and photograph them and the habitat. Often we think close-ups make the best photographs, but many other composition opportunities are possible.

From a distance you can see the animal's dominate behavioral traits: how often it raises its head, smells the air for scents and looks around. Watch to see where it has come from and where it is going. Try to determine its pace. General knowledge about wildlife always comes in handy. For instance, browsing animals such as those

in the deer family often feed facing into the wind, so they can pick up the scent of predators. Such information, along with knowing the strength and direction of the wind, can help you anticipate the direction animals will move and the point of intersection. You want to meet so you will not be photographing into the sun. Side light and back light are preferred.

The wind's strength and direction play a big part as to whether an animal detects your presence. Be aware of updrafts and downdrafts, crosswinds and swirling winds. Keep your scent away from the subject. One of the best ways to ensure that wildlife does not pick up a scent is to try to have the wind in your face while moving toward an animal. The stronger the wind, the less likely the animal will detect your scent. Never wear cologne or perfumes in the wild; unnatural scents are carried long distances and announce your presence.

Keep out of the direct sight of wildlife. Walk out of sight just below a ridge or behind a thicket of vegetation. Walk quietly in a large semicircle or crawl along behind a stone hedgerow. Do whatever it takes to stay out of sight while moving closer. Your clothing should blend with the surroundings (see "What to wear"). Remain unseen, unheard and unsmelled if you expect to get close enough to get a good photograph.

The need for photo regulations

We all should know that public land management policies have been implemented first for the perpetuation of ecosystems and for the protection of wild animals and, second, for the people who visit them.

Unfortunately, the policies have caused friction at times between photographers and the managers of public lands primarily because of a lack of understanding of each other's intentions and purposes. Most conflicts could have been avoided or prevented if photographers had followed sound environmental ethics and proper photographic protocol.

As a result of these unfortunate confrontations, the Association of Media Photographers (ASMP) and the National Park Service have worked out a mutually

NPS Commercial Photography Regulation

It is the policy of the National Park Service (NPS) to permit and encourage photography within the National Park System to the fullest extent possible consistent with the protection of resources and the enjoyment of visitors.

As a general rule, permits are not required for either commercial or noncommercial photographers. This is true whether or not the photographer uses tripods, flashbulbs, strobe lights, or interchangeable lenses.

Permits can be required when the photography involves product or service advertisement of the use of models, sets or props, or when such photography could result in damage to the resources or significant disruption of normal visitor uses. Permits shall be required for photographers granted access to areas normally closed to the visiting public except that oral approval can be given for such access to a photographer engaged in bona fide news-gathering activities.

Photographers should not need a permit to go anywhere that members of the public are generally allowed to go without a permit. Nor should a permit be needed for photographers to do anything that members of the public are generally allowed to do without a permit.

If a photography permit is deemed appropriate in any particular situation, NPS personnel should impose only those conditions necessary to accomplish the needed resource protection, visitor use or legal limitation. For advertising photography, it is appropriate to impose a permit condition that prohibits implied or stated service endorsement of the advertised product or service.

Care should be taken that conditions be reasonable. Liability insurance requirements and other limitations should not be made unduly burdensome.

National Park Service
U.S. Department of the Interior

agreed–upon general understanding for photography. If you plan to photograph in the National Park System areas, even if you are not a professional, become familiar with this agreement and carry a copy with you. If you follow all the regulations, you will not need a permit. If you plan to deviate from them, you will have to apply for a permit. The U.S. Forest Service and the Bureau of Land Management also have issued similar photography guidelines (see page 49).

Using blinds

If there is no available natural cover, carry a pocket blind or portable blind. Some pocket blinds weigh only 2.25 pounds and cover only you and the camera. Others, such as the portable Ultimate blind, are larger with room inside to lay out equipment and work with a second person. The Ultimate blind, from L.L. Rue, weighs only 9.5 pounds and can be erected in less than 30 seconds.

As a place to hide, natural cover works just as well as any blind. If you can hide behind a large tree, rock outcropping or a thicket, you successfully can observe and photograph wildlife without being noticed. The major advantage of a blind is knowing you have a place to hide instead of having to find cover and knowing you are covered totally. Nature does not guarantee perfect cover.

Either way, sit still and make no noise, because an animal can quickly detect your presence without seeing you. Wait for the animal to come within photographic range, then focus and expose your film.

Determining where to set up a blind takes work and planning, but the more you know about an animal's behavior, signals, clues, natural requirements and habitat, the better your chances of picking the right location. Take special care when locating a blind in sensitive areas or places where animals often to feed, mate, or raise their young. In such important habitats,

Many photographic images have been taken from car windows. Automobiles can work well, not only as a blind, but as a place to protect the viewer or photographer from skunks and other animals. C

erect your blind off to one side. Study the lay of the land and make sure you have a clear vantage point for observation. Set up your blind so you have optimum lighting for photographing and so the predominate winds blow from the subject toward you.

Set up a blind only when the animals are not present. To photograph birds feeding, set up your blind while they are roosting and not on their feeding grounds. Locate blinds near bird nests while they are away feeding.

For very skittish and elusive animals, such as those that live in dens or burrows, slowly introduce the blind. On the first day, set up your blind a good distance from where you anticipate photographing. On day two, move the blind a little closer. On day three, move it a little closer yet. Slowly move the blind closer toward the den or burrow, so the animal can become accustomed to it. If you move in too close too fast, you may chase off wildlife.

Auto photography

Many great wildlife photographs come from automobile windows. A car can be a photographic blind for two primary reasons: First, you can cover a greater distance by car than by foot; and second, ani-

USFS, BLM Photography Permits

In public lands administered by the U.S. Forest Service (USFS) and the Bureau of Land Management (BLM), a permit for still photography is required only in rare and unusual circumstances. These include:

●When commercial photographers take pictures of public land users, such as those engaged in recreational activities, with the express purpose of selling the pictures of those same users.

●When the photography features a commercial product for sale using the public lands as background (such as magazine advertisements).

●When the photography would have an adverse impact on the public lands, such as potential deterioration to archeological and historic features.

When these exceptions occur, the agencies may require payment of a use fee to recover administrative costs. We emphasize that this policy allows most photography to occur without permits and fees. We do request that commercial photographers contact the local USFS or BLM office to advise the agencies of their activity. We appreciate it when captions identify the public land and its location in published photographs.

It is the responsibility of the agencies, as mandated by law and regulation, to administer all activities by private entities, including commercial photographic enterprises, in a fair and equitable manner. Fees for the use of the public's land and resources will be assessed when special circumstances occur. The USFS and the BLM support and encourage photographers to make maximum use of the scenic beauty of the nation's public lands.

Forest Service
U.S. Department of Agriculture

Bureau of Land Management
U.S. Department of the Interior

A good pair of binoculars or telephoto lens will allow us to get "close" to our subject without having to be close. This northern saw-whet owl was photographed from a blind with an 800mm lens C

mals are more accustomed to automobiles than to people and often do not consider a moving vehicle a threat. It is often only when we get out of a vehicle that an animal becomes aware of us.

If you spot an animal while driving by, continue on the road until you are out of the animal's sight and earshot. Then, turn around and slowly head back. By doing so, the animal is less likely to flee than if you had stopped quickly in the first place. In some cases, lighting may be better from the other direction anyway.

If possible, stop at least 200 feet before an animal's location. Sit still for a time in the car without making any quick movements or loud noises. Turn the radio off and do not open the door so the animal can become accustomed to the auto and resume its natural behavior. After a time, when you are sure it has become accustomed to the car, ease your way forward.

When driving in the field, carry a window-mounted tripod. Have all of your basic photographic equipment loaded and readily accessible. There is nothing more frustrating than having a lens, film or mounting bracket locked in the trunk.

Window-mounted tripods hold large lenses steady while you compose images. If you do not have a window tripod, put a bean bag or a crumpled shirt across the edge of the window. Remember to turn off the engine so idling vibrations do not blur your images.

With a little practice, you can turn your automobile into an ideal mobile photographic blind.

Photographic strategies

When photographing wildlife, carry at least a 400mm lens with a 1.4X and a 2X apochromatic extender, so you will have different focal length lenses with a minimal amount of equipment to carry. The 400mm lens then can function as a 400mm, 560mm or 800mm lens depending on your needs.

By using longer lenses you can get close to a subject without physically getting close. You can full-frame a subject from 100 feet with an 800mm lens. With a standard 50mm lens you would have to be eight feet away from a subject to proportionately capture the same sizes in an image. With longer lenses, consider using a mono or tripod, so you can balance and hold a camera system steady while focusing and exposing film. When approaching an animal, try to have the sun at your back or side while facing the animal for the best photographic lighting. If you come upon an animal species you have never photographed before, take shots from a greater distance than you would prefer. You never know how long an animal will linger, so stop periodically and take insurance frames. Film is the least expensive part of any trip, so you might as well document the animal even if you do not end up with outstanding photographs. It is better to have a long shot of an animal than a shot of its disappearing tail.

Telephoto lenses vs. short lenses

Just as no wildlife viewer should be without binoculars, no amateur or experienced wildlife photographer should be without a telephoto lens. Those in the 200 to 400mm focal length are most common.

If you can get the same photographic image or see the same detail from 100 feet as from 25 feet, why move closer and unnecessarily stress the animal, trample habitat and possibly endanger yourself? Getting close to wildlife does not translate

into getting a better look or photograph. Often the opposite occurs.

Equipment to take on a trip

You cannot always take every piece of photographic equipment you own on a trip because of space and weight limitations. Carry only what you really need. Zoom lenses are often the best because they cover a variety of distances and limit the number you have to take to do the same job. Here is a list of recommended equipment:
- **Two camera bodies**—Always have a spare camera body in case one malfunctions, especially in remote areas. Put new batteries in before you leave and take an extra set with you.
- **Macro lens**—Necessary for great close-up photography.
- **Wide angle**—21mm to 35mm for landscape photograph.
- **Standard lens**—35mm to 70mm for everyday/people photography
- **Short Telephoto**—70mm to 300mm for close animal photography
- **Telephoto**—400mm and beyond for distant wildlife photography
- **1.4X and 2X**—Extenders or multipliers enable you to increase the focal length of a lens by the X factor, for example, a 400mm lens with a 2X becomes an 800mm lens.

Near or Far, Which is Best?

The following chart illustrates the differences between physically approaching a wild creature and approaching through the use of a telephoto lens or binoculars:

Physically Close	Safe Distance Viewing
• Animals experience stress	• Animals experience no stress
• Trampling of habitat	• No habitat disturbance
• Natural behavior modified	• Natural behavior unimpeded
• Image of stressed animals	• Image of relaxed animals
• Short lens increases depth of field; subject may blend with background	• Long lens decreases depth of field, separating subject from background
• Minimum time to compose image	• Maximum time to compose image
• Potential of being hurt	• Minimal chance of being hurt

If you can see it, you can photograph it. Use fast film (400 ASA or higher) for photographing in low light conditions and ASA 100 for sunny conditions.

*A tripod will also help still any possible camera movement associated with longer exposures that are required in low light conditions.*W

● **Tripod**—A sturdy tripod allows you to mount and hold your camera system still while photographing; it also forces you to compose your images.

● **Cover**—Under adverse weather conditions, a piece of canvas or plastic helps keep the elements off your cameras; in dusty areas carry a plastic bag for storage.

● **Filters**—A polarizer for your most used landscape lens will enhance images taken in midday light.

● **Film**—Carry a minimum of three rolls of 36-exposure film per shooting day, more in areas with high concentrations of wildlife and outstanding scenic views. It is always better to have too much than too little. Have a variety of different film speeds (ASA) in case the lighting changes significantly; 100 ASA for sunny conditions, 400 ASA for overcast days and early and late shooting.

● **Pack**—You also will need a camera vest, photo bag, or photo-backpack to carry gear. And do not forget a lens cloth.

● **Binoculars**—You will greatly enhance your outdoor experiences by using binoculars. Invest in a good pair. Cost varies depending on the power, range of vision, and quality. Serviceable binoculars can be obtained for about the cost of a night out on the town. For more advanced viewing, consider purchasing a wildlife spotting scope. In either case, you will be glad you made the purchase.

When traveling with your family or others, consider having binoculars for each person. It never fails, everybody wants to see the same thing at the same time. Binoculars are a simple gift but will last your child or spouse a lifetime. They make all outings enjoyable and rewarding.

Improved Experiences

While viewing and photographing wildlife may seem like benign acts, a study at the J.N. "Ding" Darling National Wildlife Refuge confirmed that such subtle actions can have a disruptive effect on wildlife and their habitats and revealed the most disruptive kinds of behavior. By avoiding these behaviors, visitors can reduce their impact, ultimately giving everyone an improved experience.

The refuge is one of the top ten birding areas in North America. This distinction, along with its tropical location on Sanibel Island, Florida, has led to its tremendous popularity with the public. An estimated 750,000 people visit the refuge each year, and more than 520,000 of them travel the five-mile wildlife drive. The high visitation sparked concerns about possible negative effects on wildlife.

Addressing these concerns, Mary Klein conducted a study that uncovered some disturbing behavior patterns. She made her observations on parts of wildlife drive where the heaviest concentrations of people and wildlife occurred and found certain human activities were responsible for displacing waterbirds from foraging habitat. The most disruptive activities included approaching wildlife too closely, throwing objects, and feeding and touching wildlife. Photographers were the most frequent offenders.

Although most people would never intentionally harm animals, visitors often are not conscious of how their actions have an impact on wildlife. Birds and other animals need energy to survive, migrate, and care for their young. It is essential for people to understand their actions can reduce an animal's limited energy supply, thus jeopardizing its chance of survival.

By responding to the distress signals—such as vocalizations and subtle movements—that animals use to communicate with each other, people can avoid disturbing wildlife and help sustain wildlife populations. This will enable us to minimize our impact so that we can continue to enjoy viewing wildlife in wild places.

Louis S. Hinds, III
Refuge Manager
J.N. "Ding" Darling National Wildlife Refuge

Truth Behind the Image

In a free press society, the editors of respected publications know they need to tell the truth, because untruthful or misleading information causes readers to lose faith in the publication. That delicate fabric of trust between reader and editor is very difficult to repair when torn.

What I see increasing throughout the media (magazines, newspapers, calendars, posters, and other forms) is that the general public is being misled by some of today's popular wildlife photography. Controlled nature photographs—whether of captive animals outdoors or of animals staged in a studio—have a long history, but their numbers seem to have increased sharply in the past 10 years. Even more recently, the altering of photos through electronics has come to be within the price range of many photographers.

Finding real wildlife can be difficult for both photographers and just plain nature lovers. Given today's highly competitive business climate, nature photographers are realizing their time has become more important. Instead of spending weeks in the wild, many of them find it much easier and far less time-consuming to photograph animals on game ranches, rehabilitation centers, and other places of captivity. Many of their photos are certainly striking, and some would not have been possible to obtain in the wild.

The use of captives is positive in the sense that it reduces some of the people-pressure on the wild populations. The resulting photographs offer the public close-up views of animals, especially rare wildlife, that otherwise may not have been possible. Also, digital enhancement can indeed improve an image artistically.

But such use also has a negative side. Some of the behavior and locations shown are not realistic; they are not found in the wild. And with the published photos, the reader often gets no indication the animals or situations are not wild, or that the photos have been electronically altered.

This situation occurs because most people are not wildlife biologists or photographers; they do not know some photos are unrealistic stagings, and they would not recognize a captive-animal portrait or a digitally altered image. Photo buyers strive to present ever-more-striking photos of animals and nature. The upshot: they are using more non-wild images.

The public can get a distorted view of nature from seeing a steady fare of these photos. And, thinking the photos were taken in the wild, amateur photographers may try to get such images themselves and go in quite close to wildlife. They may not only disturb the animals but put themselves in genuine danger.

Most editors and researchers, especially of smaller publications and textbooks, are not aware of this problem. They just want to present the best photos possible to their audience and do not always pay attention to how those photos are labeled. But buyers need to be more aware of their responsibility to their audience on this subject and not mislead them. They should offer brief explanations or symbols somewhere near the photos indicating how certain wildlife images were made: in captivity, under controlled conditions, with staged behavior, in controlled habitat, or electronically altered. Readers and viewers then would know these photos are to be enjoyed for the images they are, not necessarily as portrayals of real nature.

This truth-in-labeling process starts with photographers. They have a duty to offer this essential information at the time of submitting photos, and not wait to be asked. They may lose an occasional sale, as when an editor needs a truly wild shot. But by being forthright about their work, they maintain integrity, because buyers will know them as being trustworthy and honest. Truth and good faith pay off.

John Nuhn
Photo Editor
National/International Wildlife Magazines
National Wildlife Federation

Accepting Wild Wildlife

Yellowstone National Park offers unique opportunities to view wild animals in their natural habitats. Many species live near roads and developed areas where they are particularly observable. Animals find the best feeding opportunities in the very places we find the most attractive; this sets up many opportunities for conflict.

On a normal summer day in Yellowstone, any visitor can encounter ground squirrels and magpies being fed by hand, elk being surrounded by crowds of admiring visitors, children posing within a few feet of bison for "that perfect photo for the family album," and coyotes begging along the roadside.

In winter, coyotes, ravens, and gray jays have discovered that snowmobilers keep their lunches in the pockets on the backs of snowmobile seats. Most of them have not yet mastered opening hook and loop closures, however, so the seat receives ample damage from pecking, pawing, and gnawing.

The irony of this is that most of us visit national parks and other special places to see wild animals. Yet many of us cannot resist changing the wild nature of creatures with our handouts and close approaches. We need to begin to accept wild places and their inhabitants on their own terms. We can experience animals at close range and in unnatural settings elsewhere. There is only one Yellowstone; it is a place like nowhere else.

The National Park Service has established regulations in Yellowstone to protect wildlife. These regulations provide a framework upon which we can build a wildlife ethic for Yellowstone:

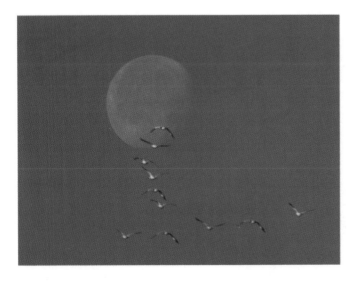

The only constant is change. A species is born, grows, gives birth and dies. Seasons also change. Some species hibernate, others, like these snow geese, migrate.

• **Resist the temptation to feed**—Handouts make wildlife vulnerable to injury by pranksters and to collisions with vehicles. Human food may cause health problems. Animals become aggressive when fed and have injured park visitors.

• **Avoid stressing wildlife**—We may choose to backpack or go camping for a week's vacation. Those creatures who live there are not on vacation. They make their living by finding food, shelter, and water as best they can. It is our responsibility to respect those whose struggles are not optional. In Yellowstone, approaching on foot within 100 yards of bears or within 25 yards of bison, elk, bighorn sheep, deer, moose, or coyotes is prohibited. Before you visit, pace off those distances with your family, so everyone has a feel for that space. Remember, animals have a sense of personal space just as we do. Suppose you are at home, eating a nice dinner in your dining room and a group of bison come in with cameras. They walk up to your table and take close and personal photos of you and your family. They walk between you and your children. How would you react? Is this really any different from one of our families approaching a herd of bison grazing in a meadow? This sort of empathy can go far toward a more respectful approach to wildlife.

• **Avoid the "tame" image**—Habituated wildlife often mislead us. They appear quite docile and tame but are still wild and unpredictable. Keep your distance and remind others to do so as well.

We encourage people to enjoy Yellowstone's wildlife. We ask only that it be done with care and respect. Our national parks are symbols of our wildlife heritage. The forethought of past generations has given us the Yellowstone we experience today; our care today can assure the same for future generations.

Sandra Snell-Dobert
Norris District Naturalist
Yellowstone National Park

Wildlife in Today's World

It's the weekend. You hop in your car and head for the woods to take wildlife photos. After a long trek through the wilderness, you return home without seeing even a rabbit.

Let's face it. You are far removed from your ancestors who knew all the tricks to approaching animals in the wild. Every animal in the forest saw, smelled, and heard you coming, and they simply stayed out of your way.

There are easier ways to photograph animals in the wild. Shrinking animal habitats and extensive study of wildlife mean we know quite a bit about where all the animals are and when they will be there. With this knowledge, you can plan to be at the right place at the right time for incredible photos.

Animals think of us as fellow animals. If you try to creep up on them or hide, they know you are there. They associate your behavior with that of a predator and leave. The way to solve this problem is to photograph wildlife from a designated viewing area. If you are standing where they expect people to be, they go about their business and ignore you. Experience has told them such people are harmless. National parks, wildlife refuges, and even major highways have designated wildlife viewing areas near known gatherings of animals.

Another good way to approach wildlife is in a car. Animals have grown accustomed to those big, noisy, smelly creatures that cannot venture from the given path. As long as you stay in your car, animals will ignore you. But step outside and you become a threat. The animal does what it usually does, it leaves. By getting out of the car, you not only ruin your own chances of getting good photographs, but you ruin opportunities for others who know enough to stay inside. Many wildlife areas have roads that are planned so they take you where animals are likely to feed or congregate. With a telephoto lens you can take outstanding wildlife photos from the comfort and convenience of your car.

Taking successful wildlife photos in today's world does not require you to actually trek into the wilderness. You simply need to know where to go, when to go, and where the viewing areas are located. It is easier on both you and the animals.

Nadine Orabona
Editor/Publisher
Photo Traveller Newsletter

Understanding Animal Behavior

We hear a lot about photographers harassing wildlife, and it happens. I had one photographer say to me, "You wait for something to happen; I make it happen." I'm sorry, that's not my style.

Harassment is defined differently by different people. Much of what is called harassment is basic animal behavior. I was given a paper in one natural area listing the types of animal behavior considered to be caused by harassment and for which you could be cited by a ranger. One rule stated none of the larger animals could be approached closer than 150 feet. That's fine; I've always advocated using at least a 400mm lens for photographing elk, moose, pronghorn, caribou, and other large animals.

Another rule stated that if you caused an animal to raise its head, it was considered harassment. Any prey animal, such as elk and caribou, that does not constantly raise its head is not going to live long enough to be big enough to be worthwhile photographing. Eternal vigilance is the price of life, and all wildlife—even big bears—raise their heads constantly to check their surroundings for potential danger.

One rule stated if an animal moves off, its action can be considered harassment. Browsing and grazing animals move constantly while feeding. It is nature's way of preventing over-utilization of a particular plant. A few nips here, a few nips there, and the animal moves. The few nips act as pruning and stimulate more plant growth. Heavy feeding on any plant destroys its reproductive capabilities, thereby destroying the plant.

Prey species move constantly and often into the wind. They move so any predator stalking them also has to move more to keep up with them. The more the predator is forced to move, the greater the chance of its being discovered.

One rule stated if an animal raises its tail, that could be considered harassment. Animals cannot defecate without raising their tails, and deer, elk, and caribou defecate on the average of 36 times in a 24-hour period; that means raising their tails at least once every 45 minutes.

If an animal gets up from its bed, that could be considered harassment, according to another rule. We are told by sleep experts that we humans roll over or move about on the average of 28 times in an eight-hour sleep period. Well, so do animals. They constantly shift positions and arise, stretch, and lie down again during their periods of rest and cud-chewing. Most animals can defecate while lying down, but some wait until they get up to do so. Most animals urinate as frequently, if not more, than they defecate. They cannot urinate while lying down. Do not photograph an animal as soon as it arises because, although standing still, it probably is urinating. Such photos don't sell well.

Most big-game animals are photographed during the rutting season because the bulls and bucks are their magnificent best. It is next to impossible to harass these animals at this time, because they are in almost constant motion and turmoil. We are lucky to keep them in sight.

We need to define what the creatures might consider harassment, not what some people might call it.

Leonard Lee Rue III
Professional Photographer and Freelance Writer

Redefine and Reinvigorate

Rightly or wrongly, the term "nature photography" has come to mean any photograph of the natural world that shows no sign of human influence. In many nature photo contests, in fact, that is the rule. Even when it is not spelled out, however, there is always this implication of prejudice against anything in an image of nature that remotely suggests the existence of human beings.

This estrangement of humans from the natural world probably began with the industrial revolution. Since then, people have become less dependent on, and aware of, their natural surroundings while simultaneously becoming more dependent on their technology. They have forgotten technology is wholly dependent on a continuing consuming need to extract resources from the natural world in ever-increasing quantities. In short, this estrangement of human beings from the natural world has led to much of the world's current environmental degradation.

In such circumstances, nature has become not "the real world" but a fenced off, separated, isolated, and estranged reservation from the real world that is now defined as "the world of humans." These reservations have names like Yellowstone, Everglades, and Denali, and photographers who spend their lives working there come to be seen by others not so much as fellow professionals but more as people from the "reservation."

Within the profession, this separation has isolated nature photographers from their colleagues. The December 1993 special issue of American Photo listed "The 100 Most Important People in Photography." Despite the ever-increasing public appetite for nature images, only one of those listed photographed nature, while more than 20 were either fashion or celebrity photographers.

The perverse irony of nature photography is that by embracing an esthetic tradition that dictates that evidence of humans shall never enter their work, nature photographers are not only deepening this schism between themselves and their non-nature colleagues, but they also may be contributing indirectly, through practices that continue to uphold the estrangement of human and natural worlds, to the very environmental crises they seek fervently to reverse through their photographic work.

It is time to readmit the human species back into nature, and it is time for nature photographers to redefine what that newly reenfranchised natural world is for the benefit of all. The goal should be to eliminate the perception that any tangible difference exists. When nature photographers succeed in picturing a world in which human beings play their vital role alongside all other life, they will have taken a giant leap toward achieving this goal.

The term "nature photography," perceived as being devoted to photographs completely lacking any suggestion of human existence, is no longer appropriate. The field of nature photography should instead be redefined as environmental photography.

As a group, environmental photography will reach far beyond the existing limits of nature photography to encompass as many of those involved in the photographic coverage of the great debate on our environment as possible.

Roger Archibald
Freelance Environmental
Writer/Photographer

Tools to Minimize Your Presence

We have come a long way in what we feel is proper ethical interaction with the natural subjects that we view, photograph, or paint. In the last century, John James Audubon routinely shot his bird subjects so he could paint in fine details as accurately as possible. In a time when the last of the American wilderness remained to be tamed and America's natural resources were being exploited, this was considered acceptable behavior. Shoot a passerine today, however, and it not only could cost you heavy fines but land you in jail.

So what is acceptable behavior when interacting with wildlife? The goal is minimal impact, which actually benefits both the subject and photographer. The creature does not get unduly stressed, and the photographer gets an opportunity to observe and to capture on film its behavior uninterrupted by the presence of man.

Knowledge of both your subject and of the specialized outdoor photographic equipment available today is the key to obtaining great wildlife photographs without scaring away and/or stressing your subject.

Most wildlife photography is done while the photographer's presence is known to the subject, but the subject may be wary, small in size, or too dangerous for the photographer to approach closely. This makes the telephoto lens an indispensable tool for the wildlife photographer. Too often, in places like Yellowstone National Park, I have observed tourists approaching large animals, such as bison and elk, with point and shoot cameras with 35mm or 50mm lenses. To record a decent size image on the film, they are forced to approach too closely. This not only harasses the animals but puts the photographer's own life in danger.

It is important to know how dangerous and fast the animals can be and to know your equipment's limitations. With proper knowledge, you will be better able to determine safe distances from the subject and choose the right lens for the high–quality image that you seek.

Another valuable tool for obtaining full-frame, high-quality images of wildlife is the blind. In Europe, this tool is called a photographic hide, a most appropriate term because that is exactly how it is used. With human presence hidden, animals go about normal activities, which you can observe and capture on film. Sometimes in a blind you can get full images of customarily wary subjects that you might not even get with an 800mm lens.

A third useful tool is a long-range release for triggering motor-drive cameras. This tool allows you to have your camera close to the subject while you stay back to minimize your presence. Cameras can be triggered from afar either by a long electric cable or by radio remote. This type of setup most commonly is used when a subject returns time and again to the same spot, such as when a bird is attending to young in a nest.

By utilizing these photographic tools, you will have more enjoyable and successful photographic shoots. If John James Audubon had had access to today's modern photographic equipment, he might have used a camera instead of a gun.

Len Rue Jr.
Professional Photographer and Freelance Writer

This moose family clearly creates and portrays a single subject. W

Basics Elements for Good Images

"A joy shared is a joy doubled."
—Goethe

The camera does not matter nearly as much as the person behind it. People are responsible for taking great pictures, not cameras. You are the person behind the camera who composes the image, manipulates and utilizes light and calculates exposure.

Many professional photographers are self-taught and continue to educate themselves for they understand that many aspects are involved in producing great photographic images. A good eye for composition is a necessity, but you also need a working knowledge of the technical aspects of light, metering and exposure settings. The following basic techniques will help you become a better scenic and wildlife photographer.

Compose your image

One of the most important ingredients in a successful image is composition. What makes a pleasing image is in the eye of the beholder. When composing an image, try deliberately to direct the viewer's eye to focus on the subject matter you wish to emphasize. Seldom, if ever, does the human eye rest while observing. As it follows every line and curve, it also focuses along all perceived planes within our three dimensional perception. A well-composed image guides and directs the viewer's eye to its point of interest.

While composing your image, keep in mind that still-life photography lacks motion and depth of field. They only can be suggested through subject placement, balance, perspective, framing, scale, light and shadows. Lines, shapes and patterns tend to draw the human eye to the intersection of horizontal, vertical and diagonal lines. We tend to focus on the diversion and conversion of lines. If the placement of the intersection or the direction of the lines collectively allow your eyes to travel back to the subject, then the photograph is composed effectively.

Creating a pleasing composition starts when you look through the viewfinder. Deliberately move your camera around and place your subject to the left or the right, perhaps slightly higher or lower than center. Expose as you go. After your film has been developed, study your images. See what composition works best. Soon you will be on your way to creating properly composed images.

One subject per image

A good photograph speaks to its viewers without explanation. Try to include only one subject per image so the viewer will see clearly what you are trying to portray. A single subject does not necessarily mean one object. It may consist of related elements such as a mountain range, a field of flowers, a herd of animals, a flock of birds, predator/prey interaction or even a stand of trees.

Keep your background simple. Complex and busy backgrounds compete with the subject for the viewer's attention. Unrelated background elements create clutter and a lack of cohesiveness. By keeping an image simple, you achieve a stronger effect. The more background objects that appear in your photo, the weaker it becomes, because the eye is unable to focus on one central point of interest.

Many times unwanted objects happen to end up in pictures. To minimize clutter and unruly backgrounds, deliberately look past the subject before pressing the shutter release. If you see any unwanted and unre-

*The snow-covered fence line draws the eye into the photograph, creating a depth of field, while the centered owl creates a point of focus.*C

lated features in your viewfinder, change your position so the subject appears against a less obtrusive background. Be especially careful to exclude cars, telephone poles, wires and other photographers. A good way to clean up and enhance a background in nature photography is to assume a somewhat low position and photograph your subject against the sky.

Do not be afraid to use film.

Experiment with backgrounds and enhance your skills.

Keep it. tight A subject that does not cover a large enough proportion of an image cannot capture the viewer's attention. In essence, a subject that is too small will not create an exciting image. It will be overpowered by extraneous elements.

A general rule of thumb is that your subject should occupy a minimum of 25 percent of the total viewfinder frame to create an effective image. Look through your viewfinder, calculate the percentage of the total area your subject occupies, and, if necessary, move closer to your subject. When photographing wildlife, however, use telephoto lenses instead of moving closer in most situations.

Strengthening your wildlife image

Make your subject look alive. Vary the time of day you shoot and the angle and length of lens you use. Photograph wildlife when it is alert and active. Usually that means early or late in the day. Attempt to capture highlights in an animal's eyes and reflections off the antlers or off their hair or feathers. Look for movement that creates the suggestion of power. Try capturing natural behavior such as an animal feeding or cleaning itself. These images look alive.

When photographing wild creatures, do so at eye level or slightly lower. Try to photograph wildlife looking at or past the camera. These images create a sense of communication.

By utilizing a longer lens you can tighten up on a subject without having to move closer. A good rule of thumb to remember is that a subject should occupy at least 25 percent of the picture. C

Vary your viewpoint

Most photography is done from a standing photographer's eye level and results in an endless string of generic images. Consider how pleasing an image of a child would be if it were taken at his/her eye level instead of looking down on the child. The same applies to wild animals and plants. Consider photographing a flower silhouetted against the sky as opposed to an overhead view of it in the grass. Changing your vantage point creates a new perspective and suggests energy and creativity in your photographs.

Rhythm and reflections

Utilize rhythmic patterns in nature to create a mood in scenic or in wildlife photography. They might be repeating colors, shapes, or objects. For instance, ripples created by throwing a stone in a pond are a rhythmic pattern. A line of trees, a school of fish, or reflected light can create rhythm in a photograph. Look for them to help you create more interesting images.

Utilize reflections in nature to create special effects or moods. When photographing a puddle, try to pick up reflected tree branches. At a lake, capture the reflection of shoreline trees or mountain backdrop. If the water is absolutely motionless, a mirror image is created. Ripples distort reflections and create an entirely different mood suggesting motion and energy. Both create a good depth of field.

Available light

Midday light or light shining directly down on a subject is harsh and difficult to work with, so photos taken in midday often look flat.

Side light is the most dramatic of all natural lights. Side light strengthens an image, creating shadows. Shadows from the top and side accentuate form and texture. When shadows are incorporated into your photography, they create a more artistic image with a perceived increased

Above: Capture your subject doing something; make it look alive. Action shots are always impressive especially ones in which your subject is coming towards you, such as this screech owl. C

Right: A red tailed hawk alights in full splendor. Only through understanding the behavior of birds can we hope to view and achieve photographic images of them doing what they do naturally.. C

depth of field. The lower the angles of light, the greater the natural shadows. This early-day and late-day soft light creates a warming of natural colors and tones and both become increasingly more dramatic as the shadows lengthen.

Side-lighted images almost always catch the viewer's eye even if detail is lacking in the shadows. Side light is the most important light when trying to capture texture and form, color saturation and tonality.

Back light, or light behind your subject, accentuates a subject's contours and often produces dramatic silhouetted images.

Defused light produced by overcast skies creates soft colors and allows details to filter into shadowed areas. Heavy overcast, cloud–covered and rain-filled skies create somber moods.

The more film you shoot, the more likely you are to improve your photography. Experiment with composition, lighting, exposure and backgrounds. The only thing you have to lose is film. As you review your photography, you will begin to see what works and what does not work. Each photographic chance not taken or not experimented with is a missed opportunity to get a spectacular shot and to improve your skills.

Good scenic photography takes a great deal of time and work. Carefully frame your subject and wait for the lighting to be just right. W

Part Three: Specific Tips

Scenic Areas

"There is nothing so American as our parks. The scenery and wildlife are native. The fundamental idea behind the parks is native."
—Franklin Delano Roosevelt

Scenic areas are the single most photographed natural subjects. Truly fine scenic photography takes a great deal of time, work and planning. With different seasons and different weather conditions, the sunlight changes greatly and affects the appearance of a landscape.

I drive the same road by the same woods each day to drop off and pick up my daughter at day care. Most of the time the woods look like a regular old patch of trees, but there are days when the woods look more alive and vibrant. One day the early morning light dances off the morning mist, creating smoky shafts of light that capture my eye. Another day the autumn colors seem extra special in the late afternoon sun. In the winter, with the leaves off the trees and snow covering the understory, the woods takes on a stark purity.

Most people expect scenic areas to be overwhelming and grand, and they want to capture everything in a single picture. All too often, however, these beautiful landscapes are so massive that a single image cannot do them justice. A scene may be grand and awesome but not necessarily photogenic. Another scene, like my patch of woods, might be commonplace but photogenic in many ways.

When you are photographing in scenic areas, keep these factors in mind:

Perspective

Your vantage point, or perspective, will greatly change the look of any landscape. For instance, if you photograph from a high angle, the captured image will tend to create a feeling of a shortened perspective, which sometimes crowds a subject. This perspective might be good for depicting herds of animals and flocks of birds but not mountains or seascapes. A low perspective, on the other hand, will enhance the feeling of a greater depth of field and capture the expanse of vast landscapes.

Change lenses to affect perspective instead of changing locations and possibly trampling an area. Many excellent scenic photos are photographed with long lenses. Two objectives can be accomplished with long lenses: you can flatten or compress the elements together and/or you can selectively extract smaller scenes from the whole. Long lenses often are used to make sand dunes appear closer together.

Framing

The use of framing in scenic foregrounds also changes an image's perspective by adding a sense of a greater depth of field. A scenic picture with a neutral or empty foreground often is not as effective as one with an interesting foreground with such features as tree branches, foliage, rock outcroppings, and even fences. They help enhance and strengthen an image with a feeling of detail. Subtle framing creates a truer three-dimensional perception in an

It's Alive: Cryptobiotic Soil

It may look like dirt, but it's not. It's alive. It's cryptobiotic soil. Cryptobiotic soil looks like soft, lumpy mineral soil with a dark thin crust, but it is a self-sustaining macrobiotic soil unique to arid uplands. This biological unit is a combination of lichens and mosses that reproduces via spores instead of by seeds as flowering plants reproduce. These organisms require little nutrition and grow on seemingly barren ground.

Cryptobiotic soils are a critical part of the soil-building process in arid regions, because they act as anti-erosional and nitrogen-enriching agents and prepare the ground for a succession of plant growth.

Although these soils may be quite common in many desert areas, they also are extremely fragile. A mature cryptobiotic garden may take 50 to 100 years to develop and can be easily damaged by a single footstep or bicycle track.

image and conveys an illusion of being able to step right into the image.

Foreground subjects not only draw but engage the viewer's attention in the image. Classic S curves in a sand dune, for example, pull the viewer into the scene. Ansel Adams was the master of near/far perspectives. For example, he would compose with boulders in the foreground leading the viewer's eye in and to a mountain peak.

Scale

Sometimes include people, common objects or wildlife in a scenic photograph to give your viewers an idea how high a tree or waterfall might be or how broad the vista. Or, do just the opposite. Without an object for reference, you can make a tiny cascade look like a majestic waterfall. Scale is important when documenting a species or scene. If you are trying for an artistic interpretation, scale is just as important but does not have to be accurate.

Lighting

The use of light is one of the most powerful elements in capturing an image. Lighting can affect perspective, framing and scale. How you utilize light affects the mood of your image and can add a magical element to a scene. Light can enhance an object within a scene that otherwise would have gone unnoticed.

The best scenic photographic images are the ones that create a three-dimensional feeling. Such images are often saturated with pastels and rich colors created by early-morning or late-afternoon sunlight.

When you are taking a photograph of a sunrise or sunset, look also in the other direction, where the light is going. Often the best potential photographs are behind us in scenes enriched by long intense rays of light. The deep, long shadows of low light create dramatic textures in sand, trees, snow, rocks, mountains and other features. Avoid the contrast and flat light of midday when photographing scenic areas.

Different weather conditions greatly affect the mood or sentiment presented in a picture. Early morning mist, for instance, helps create beautiful, soft, moody images that seem to fade into a nothingness. Rain conjures a feeling of loneliness, while landscapes with snow may create interesting graphic lines and patterns. Look at photo postcards and greeting cards. Their mood usually is conveyed by the interplay of lights and darks in the photograph. The sun's light can help you create stunning statements of the places you love to visit.

Landscape photography is a good place to start as a photographer, but it is not necessarily easy. Excellent scenic photographs come with time, practice,

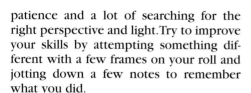

patience and a lot of searching for the right perspective and light. Try to improve your skills by attempting something different with a few frames on your roll and jotting down a few notes to remember what you did.

A different world

We take so much for granted in our daily lives. When we get up in the morning and turn on the light switch, we expect light. When we turn on the faucet, we expect water. When we turn the key in our car's ignition, we expect it to start. They are a part of our day-to-day lives.

The lights go on because of the electrician, the electrical engineers, the power lines, the power plants and much more. The water comes to us courtesy of the plumber, the fixture supplier, the pipe manufacturer, the water company or the well. All these steps are taken for granted when we drink a glass of water.

If there is even a minor problem with the electricity, plumbing or our motor vehicles, most of us do not attempt to fix it ourselves. Without any knowledge of the subject or without a comprehensive reference book, we are helpless. In most cases, we call in the experts to make sure we do not electrocute ourselves, flood our homes or destroy our vehicles.

In the natural world, we expect the sun to rise, the grass to grow, the birds to fly and the rain to fall. But do we really know any more about our natural surroundings and how they function than we know about the electricity? Probably not. Why, then, do we think we know so much about the great outdoors when we spend so little time in it? An average American spends less than 2 percent of his adult life interacting with nature, and 98 percent of his time in the worlds of electricity, plumbing, and automobiles.

Generally, we acknowledge cause-and-effect relationships in our daily lives and trust experts to guide us. But often we do not take seriously some experts we hire with our tax dollars—park, refuge, and forest managers, field biologists, naturalist interpreters and rangers. If no one is looking, for example, we bend the rules and go off the trail. We rationalize what we do by saying it will not make any difference and nothing will be affected. But such actions can make a significant difference to flora and fauna, which

Foreground subjects help frame and create a sense of depth, a three dimensional effect in a two dimensional picture. W

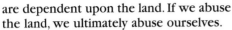

are dependent upon the land. If we abuse the land, we ultimately abuse ourselves.

Every year millions of us travel in search of nature. We have a direct impact on the landscape as we crush vegetation and spoil habitats. With a little effort we can do much to help protect scenic areas.

Stay on trails

An average adult foot in a hiking boot covers a surface 0.33 square feet. Three steps cover one square foot. Over the course of a 100–foot walk, an adult tramples 11 square feet. If 100 people walk in the same area, they crush 1,100 square feet of vegetation, an area equivalent to that of an average American home. A thousand individuals can destroy 11,000 square feet, the area of a small office building.

Our footsteps can create new trails that cover our landscapes like spider webs. Staying on designated trails is one of the simplest ways to lessen our impact on the natural world. To increase your chances of seeing wildlife, avoid stepping on sticks, dry leaves and crystallized snow. Instead, try to walk on dirt, sand and rocks while staying on the trail. Damp leaves and wet snow muffle footsteps and help to keep noise to a minimum.

For your safety and for habitat preservation, do not step on fallen logs. Any log that has been sitting for a long time is decomposing, and a person can easily crush homes of small creatures. You also can lose your footing on a log and fall, possibly hurting yourself and damaging your equipment.

Bicycling wisely

Seemingly overnight, brightly colored, lyca-clad mountain bike enthusiasts have discovered the open roads and trails of public lands. These lands offer some of the best cycling in the world by providing access to thousands of miles of backcountry trails and an opportunity to cycle without fear of automobiles.

Before you ride into an area, check to see who manages the land and read their regulations. Help take care of these public lands, they are yours. Respect all posted regulations, such as "no trespassing" or "closed due to critical habitat." Areas that are marked critical are crucial to the health, welfare and survival of one or more species.

Minimize your impact on an area by learning to avoid skidding or spinning your wheels, by practicing smooth round turns and by slowly stopping your bike. Master climbing hills without spinning your rear tire. Walk your bike around water bars, which are rock and log drains built to direct water off trails. Lifting your bike over such barriers prevents erosion. Avoid riding on extremely wet trails, because tires can leave deep ruts that channel runoff and accelerate erosion.

Many of our natural and recreational areas seem tough and durable, whereas they are actually extremely fragile and take years to recover from erosion and other problems. Those who follow you into these public lands, many of which are administered by the Bureau of Land Management, deserve to find the same pristine beauty you did. Ride wisely, so others may have great outdoor experiences, too.

Cycle Protocol

Safety and courtesy go hand and hand. Simply yelling "bike" is not enough. Here are some tips to follow when encountering:

- **Hikers** When approaching from in front or behind, make your presence known and wait until they can easily move to the side of the trail before attempting to pass; then pass slowly.
- **Horses** When approaching from behind, quietly make your presence known and ask to pass. Wait until the equestrian can find a wide enough place on the trail to step to the side safely. Then ride or walk your bike slowly by. Pull to the side of the trail when meeting head-on and avoid making any sudden movements or loud noises. Allow them to pass. Remember, your bike is not likely to bolt or stampede, but a scared horse might trample someone or damage gear.
- **Other cyclists** Downhill riders should yield to uphill riders.

Photo courtesy of Robert D. McCall.

Rock Art

While you are travelling in America's wilderness areas, particularly in the West, you may come across rock art and other ancient artifacts. Treat them with respect, for they represent the rich cultural heritage of Native Americans – and they are protected by law.

Whether pecked, incised, or painted, rock art inspires a sense of awe and reverence in most people. Many sites, however, have fallen victim to vandals wielding spray cans and to lovers carving their initials. Other sites have been damaged by people making rubbings to frame or by people simply touching them. Rock art is fragile. The delicate balance between rock and pigment can be destroyed easily.

- Be cautious where you place tripods and other photographic equipment.
- Pay attention where you step; do not trample or disturb grinding sites, rock art, or other artifacts.
- Be cautious with fire to avoid damaging rock art with smoke.
- Do not remove or reposition artifacts.
- Do not touch or make rubbings of rock art.
- Do not apply chalk, paint , water, or any substances to rock.
- Monitor children's behavior in the sacred places.

Robert D. McCall

Pack it out

In Bryce Canyon National Park, an orange peel or banana peel will last between two and five years before it disappears; a cigarette butt, 13 years; an aluminum soda or beer can, 200 to 500 years; plastic and Styrofoam, 500 or more years. An unofficial report states a biodegradable plastic trash bag can blow around for well over two years. Each environment is different and the decomposition time for any product varies.

We are all familiar with pictures of seabirds and marine mammals choking and bleeding from plastic six-pack rings. We have read or heard stories of countless marine mammals, sea turtles and whales dying because they swallowed plastic bags or balloons. Such tragedies occur even in lands far from the sea. At Grand Canyon, for example, biologists conducted autopsies on several deer that had starved to death in the national park. They found the animals' stomachs were coated and filled with undigested pieces of plastic snack bags.

Wildlife, like humans, need a certain amount of minerals, and one highly sought by deer and other ungulates is salt. Thus the deer not only licked the salt off the bags but consumed the bags in search of more salt.

To protect wildlife and to ensure those people who follow you have an enjoyable visit, take all of your trash with you and dispose of it properly. Leave no traces of your visit and pack out any trash that you find.

Backcountry hygiene

Water and washing in some ecosystems can become a bigger problem than most people realize. In arid or desert regions, for example, there are few mechanisms for replacement or purification of cumulative pollutants in the limited water supply. Overusing or misusing water may deplete supplies crucial to the survival of plants and animals. Waste water from cooking and bathing can pollute rivers and wetland areas.

Here are a few guidelines to follow so you do not contaminate water resources:

● Never bathe or wash dishes at the water source. Dispose of dirty water in vegetated areas well away from the water source.

● Use only clean cups and pots to dip from the water source.

● In river areas, pour cooking waste water directly into the river after first pouring it through a fine mesh screen to remove the larger food particles. Bag and pack out the collected food.

● Make sure you are at least 200 feet away from any side stream when washing or bathing with soap and make sure the soap you use is biodegradable.

Most people avoid talking about the disposal of human waste, but everyone has to deal with it daily in the outdoors—and not necessarily just on long overnight trips. Use portable toilets, bury it far from any water source, or it may be even necessary to pack out solid body waste in plastic bags.

Walking: wetlands and dunes

Two-thirds of the Earth's surface is covered with water, so there are millions of miles of shoreline with no real beginning or end creating an intertidal zone critical for many wildlife species. This interaction of land and sea creates extremely fertile estuary habitats, such as salt marshes and mangrove swamps, that are dependent on both fresh and salt water. At first glance, estuaries often appear to be monocultures primarily consisting of one species of vegetation, but if we take a close look, perhaps with a microscope, we find they are biologically diverse ecosystems teeming with life.

Linked by the tides, the estuary complex consisting of creeks, marshes, mud flats, river mouths and barrier islands is a single community. Tidal currents surge, bringing in water so rich that millions of minute plants and animals can be found in a single quart. This is the starting point for marine food chains in which bigger things eat little things.

The estuary's mud and its flora trap calcium, phosphorus and other elements vital to life. Decaying marsh grasses and mangroves feed microorganisms, which in turn feed on an abundance of plant life, shrimp, oysters, mussels, crabs and little fish, which are eaten by bigger fish, shorebirds, ducks, muskrats, raccoons and a multitude of other species, including man.

How we use the lands adjacent to streams, rivers, bogs, ponds, lakes, bays and oceans greatly affects the water quality and the plant and animal species within them. When we trample vegetation along streambanks, both land animals and aquatic creatures suffer in some way or are forced to leave their mating, breeding, and rearing grounds. Trampling leads to erosion and silt washes into the waterways. Over time, the silt suffocates larva, eggs, bivalves, invertebrates, crustaceans and other aquatic creatures.

Beach sand dunes may not be as rich in life as the wetlands, but they are even more fragile. Root systems of resident grasses and plants hold them together and prevent them from being washed away by water and blown away by the winds. Many shorebirds use the dunes and nearby open sands as nesting areas.

Here are a few ways to reduce erosion problems and protect fragile wetlands and dunes:
- Avoid walking on the edges of an embankment.
- Walk slightly inland, a minimum of 10

Although looked at as two different worlds, this single image reflects the fertile interface between land and water.
W

feet, and walk parallel to the water's edge. Approach the water perpendicularly. If possible, use rock outcroppings or sandy beaches to approach the water.

●Avoid walking up or downstream in the water near the banks; walk in the water five feet from the embankment and move parallel to the land.

●In open sand areas without trails, walk well away from any vegetation.

●In sand dunes, stay on designated trails. Most types of sand dune vegetation have large and expansive root systems that lie just below the sand's surface. A footstep can easily sever roots, which are holding the dunes together, so do not walk close to any plant life.

●Be alert for nests and stay out of closed critical habitats.

●Make sure your tripod legs do not damage root systems.

A Long–Felt Impact

Olympic National Park encompasses nearly one million acres of lush forests, rocky coastlines, and rugged mountains. Known as one of the last areas explored by settlers in the lower 48 states, the Olympics have long felt the impact of humans. Early Native American groups tapped the resources of the Olympic Peninsula by using everything from the western red cedar to the migrating salmon in their day-to-day lives. However, they never had an impact on the landscape like that caused by today's millions of visitors.

One of the most significant visitor impacts on the national park is the trampling of human feet. In the high country, footsteps crush vegetation not adapted to the pounding force of thousands of feet. The death of the plants exposes the thin mountain soils that soon erode. The unsightly bare ground can last for up to a century unless expensive revegetation efforts repair the damage.

Even the thick soils of the temperate rain forest are not immune to trampling. Feet crush decomposing logs that serve as homes for insects and fungi vital to forest processes. Extensive way trails and sprawling campsites compact the soil, damaging neighboring trees.

Along the rocky coastline one misplaced foot can end the life of a thousand–year-old green sea anemone. Killing or removing one member of a tidepool creates ripples throughout the entire community.

Walking on the established trails or bare rock and sand along the coast lessens the impact on the park environment. By not feeding wildlife, picking plants, removing tidepool creatures, or littering we can help preserve this varied landscape for generations to come. Olympic National Park is unique wilderness where the influence of people should not leave a lasting mark.

Dan Johnson
Naturalist Interpreter
Olympic National Park

The elongated shadows of these side-lighted buffalo add a sense of texture to an otherwise plain image. W

Feeding Wildlife

I have offered many explanations to help folks understand why they should not feed wildlife. It seems a lot of people do not care whether or not they might be bitten or even catch a disease from an animal. Reasoning that our food is not healthy for wild animals has been countered by those who propose scientifically blended "natural foods for wildlife."

My favorite stories are: "I'm not feeding it, I'm giving it water; it doesn't have anything to drink," and "I'm not feeding it, I don't have anything but these rocks" as the visitor held out his hand to lure the prairie dog to him.

A wild animal's primary job is to live long enough to reproduce. Anything we do to interfere with that job is harmful to the species. Just our presence in the area may cause wild animals to look up or move away and lose feeding time. When we approach critters or entice them to us, we interrupt their normal feeding habits. We lure them to places like roadsides where the chances of being struck by a car are greater. And if too many of us stay too long, we erode that natural wariness that protects them from other predators.

Susan Colclazer
Chief of Interpretation
Bryce Canyon National Park

The form, texture and habitat of plants, with or without flowers, provides intriguing possibilities for photographers. W

Wildflowers and Other Plants

"The earth laughs in flowers."
—Ralph Waldo Emerson

Clear, rich-blue skies were overhead and not so much as a breath of air stirred at ground level. The morning dew still hung heavy on every leaf, flower, and blade of grass. I knew that mood would not last long. With the warming rays of the day's first light, I would have to work quickly. The rich hidden colors trapped deep within the field of flowers would evaporate soon. The glistening magic would disappear.

Momentarily spellbound by the menagerie of rainbow-colored flowers, forms and textures, I gazed around thinking, "where to begin?" It all looked so beautiful. How could I capture all this splendor and beauty in one photograph? Which of the millions of possible compositions would be the ultimate one?

It is not always as easy as it sounds, but it helps to isolate sections in the mind's eye while observing the whole. When photographing plant life, try to find simple, clean, crisp compositions and lines that carry the viewer's eye into the image. The eye needs lines to follow and something to lock on. Otherwise, the eye wanders and the image is confusing and less powerful. Create an image without a lot of distracting elements that translates the feelings of that moment. What direction is best to shoot with natural available lighting? Side lighting often gives a sense of form and texture.

One flowerscape had one section with only a few isolated flowers. Looking and studying the scene while continually moving, I finally ended up lying flat on the ground in dew-covered grass staring up at the sky. What a perspective with rich, fragrant flowers against a breathtaking morning sky!

More people photograph wildflowers than any single subject in nature besides scenic landscapes because of their variety,

Getting up early and being in the field as the sun rises is a key to capturing colorful images. A different perspective will also help. W

availability and exquisite beauty. Wildflowers are much easier to capture on film than wildlife. Flowers cannot fly or run away—but too often I do find that they refuse to stand still as they weave and dance with the slightest stirring of air.

Flowers can be found almost anywhere: in city parks, along roadsides, in lawns, in a hedgerows, on stream embankments and in forests. Late spring through midsummer is the most dramatic time of year to view and photograph wildflowers. Blankets of color seem almost endless in mountain meadows and alpine slopes. Dramatic contrasts coupled with brilliant colors make for the best flower photography. Opportunities abound for capturing natural sculptures and nature's versions of impressionistic art.

Some of the hardiest flowers are buttercups, daisies and others that grow plentifully in mountain meadows and along roadsides. Delicate flowers that tend to bloom early can be found in woodlands, bogs and swamps. Plants such as the lady's-slipper, swamp pinks and sundews can be found in many parts of the country. Fireweed and other fall plants mark the end of the flowering season.

For wildflower photography, take advantage of natural light when it is at its optimum, just before sunset or after sunrise. I prefer photographing wildflowers and other plants in early morning. The dew left by the night's mist and the long rays of early sunlight enhance images. Mist and water droplets bring out and intensify rich deep colors hidden at midday when the sun is the hottest and leaves and petals are dry.

How many of us sit back and think about all the things we have done to capture a good image of a flower or fern? Many photographers have ignored regulations and have pruned or matted down grasses and weeds so they would not interfere with subjects. Camera lenses, camera bodies and bags have been used to hold back branches. Many photographers contort their bodies to hold back large branches. Instead of going to such extremes and possibly damaging vegetation, carry a small length of nylon string or cord to tie back branches.

One of the most frustrating aspects every photographer has to deal with when photographing delicate flora is subtle movement. A slight movement can cause an otherwise tack-sharp image to appear soft around the edges or even blurry. Try using your body or that of others to block breezes. It is tough to focus your camera while holding a branch and trying to block the wind. It does not work, I assure you.

A multi-purpose, collapsible reflector ring is a very handy all-around tool for any type of macro photography. The best part is that it takes up almost no space in your

A mountain meadow in midsummer can offer unlimited opportunities for great flower photography. W

camera bag or backpack. From a small eight-inch circle, about three-quarters of an inch thick, it unravels into a solid sur-faced round screen about three feet across. After securing any unwanted vege-tation, place the screen to block the opposing winds. It is that simple to use.

For just a moment, let's suppose the subject we wish to photograph is in the shade. We can use the reflector not only to block the wind but to reflect some light on the subject. If you are photographing a flower under bright midday sun, use a reflector to bounce light into shadowed sides for "fill," thereby reducing contrast. Another technique is to carry a collapsi-ble diffuser. Hold it just above the flower and use the reflector to bounce some light on the subject.

Another trick used by professionals when photographing wildflowers is to carry—in a waterproof container—a mist bottle filled with water. At midday a flower's colors often are dull and muted. To enhance the flower's appearance, spray mist onto the petals. If leaves or stems are included in the composition, spray them, too, or the photograph will give it away that you have sprayed. Like magic, the hid-den beautiful colors come to life and are accented by a water droplet. Combine the mist bottle with the reflector/diffuser techniques and again, magic!

When shooting wildflowers and plants, watch your tripod legs. They can crush other plants as your focus your attention on a specific subject. Be especially careful when spreading your tripod's legs for shooting low to the ground. Poison oak and ivy are primarily ground dwellers, and if you or your equipment touch them they can cause a rash.

Some people wear rubber boots, even chestwaders, when shooting in the morn-ing in meadows and grasslands. Dew very quickly can soak your clothing as you walk around. You will not feel very cre-ative if you are wet and shaking from cold. Hypothermia, a dangerous lowering of body temperature, also can occur under these conditions. You do not have to be in snow or high altitudes to suffer hypothermia.

Woodland and bog spring flowers, such as Arethusa, are colorful and delicate. W

There are more than 20,000 endan-gered plant species worldwide. All flora found in our national parks and national wildlife refuges is protected as a natural resource along with the wildlife. Do not pick or trample wildflowers, so they can they mature and produce seeds for the next generation of plants and to provide food for wildlife—and esthetic beauty.

Learning About Wilderness Solitude

What people commonly seek in wilderness is solitude, a chance to be apart from the intensity of daily life, a chance to be quiet, to reflect, to enjoy natural beauty.

For many persons, this means traveling alone or with a friend or two. For others, there is value to traveling in a larger group. It is commonly believed that groups traveling in the wilderness are inappropriate and disruptive. That certainly can be true, but group travel can serve the ideals of wilderness preservation and personal renewal in different and valuable ways.

Nearly everyone who travels in the backcountry has experienced arriving at a campsite to find it occupied by a group. There are times when a group will disturb the sanctity of one's wilderness experience by engaging in loud, disruptive, and otherwise inappropriate behavior. There is no question this is a problem that degrades the quality of wilderness. However, there are other times when a group will disturb other travelers by its mere presence regardless of the wilderness ethic being followed.

Some people advocate that group travel should be banned or severely limited. This is a misconception. What is bad for wilderness is impact in all its forms: land degradation, water pollution, visual and noise pollution. We go to the wilderness to escape them. But a well-managed group can have far less impact than a single careless traveler.

Groups traveling in the wilderness frequently are working toward one of two important aims. First, they are trying to foster an appreciation of wilderness and the natural world. This is the principal purpose of the Sierra Club's Outing programs, and it can be demonstrated in dozens of examples over nearly 100 years that this approach has saved the wilderness. Taking people to threatened places like the Grand Canyon, Dinosaur National Monument, and the Arctic National Wildlife Refuge has built an advocacy that is invaluable in the battle for protection. Nothing

can inspire a deeply held value like direct experience. In many cases, it is not enough to tell people the places are worth protecting or encourage them to visit them on their own. Organizations like the Sierra Club have made it their business to facilitate opportunities for people to see, experience, and understand wilderness.

A second important purpose of group travel is skills training. Organizations such as the National Outdoors Leadership School and Outward Bound offer opportunities to learn how best to travel, survive, and respect wilderness. Their approach of enhancing experience through enhancing technique serves a valuable purpose. In our world where so much value is placed on learning that serves the marketplace or career advancement, programs that teach leadership and understanding of the natural world offer an alternative intellectual pursuit that is priceless.

In both of these contexts, teaching the skills and tenets of low-impact camping is an essential part of the mission. When done properly, a group wilderness experience prepares each individual for solo experiences in the wilderness as responsible and enlightened travelers.

I would suggest that when you encounter a group in the wilderness that you reflect on the value that the experience brings to each individual and on the long-range good these programs can bring to the cause of wilderness protection. Many people do not understand proper wilderness manners, but not all, or even most, groups conduct themselves irresponsibly. They are travelers learning and seeking renewal. Expect an appropriate standard of impact, but respect this legitimate method of learning how to love the wilderness better.

John DeCock
Associate Director of Conservation
Sierra Club

Looking at the whole gives us an overview of a scene. a closer look reveals subtle hidden details. W

Sometimes we can overlook little things like this bee, a critical element in the cross-pollination of flowers. W

Insects

"If a child is to keep alive his inborn sense of wonder...he needs the companionship of at least one adult who can share it, rediscovering with him the joy, excitement and mystery of the world we live in."

—Rachel Carson

Creepy, crawly I may be, but a butterfly someday, you will see. W

Creepy, crawly, flying, biting bugs! Our first reaction to bugs is to squash them without thinking what purposes they might serve in our natural world.

Bugs are everywhere, living in every known habitat. Most animal species visible to the naked eye are insects. Approximately 10,000 new insects are discovered each year. Surprisingly, however, only a small percentage of the worldwide insect population bites people. We might question that statistic, especially when standing in a mosquito-filled salt marsh or in a freshwater swamp on a warm summer day.

Insects are vital in the web of life as primary consumees and as decomposers in many food chains. Insects pollinate plants, help decompose natural litter and provide a major food source to countless numbers of amphibians, reptiles, birds, mammals, and fishes.

Since the beginning of time, man has considered most insects mere nuisances. Written records and ledgers dating back hundreds of years tell of great plagues of insects.

More recently, in the 1920s, U.S. farmlands were consumed by insects. A decade later, President Franklin D. Roosevelt assigned Civilian Conservation Corps and Works Progress Administration workers to control mosquito populations to prevent the spread of diseases and to reduce pests. They dug ditches to drain salt marshes and freshwater meadows because mosquitoes require standing water to breed. Ditching and widespread urban and agricultural development are major contributors to the reduction of wetlands around the world.

For every action, there are multiple reactions. DDT, an insecticide, was introduced to control mosquitoes and other insects. While it reduced insects, many birds, fishes and other species ingested DDT causing tremendous losses of wildlife. Although DDT is no longer used in North America, it still is being used in numerous other countries.

We tend to judge a creature's value on its looks and our convenience. Without even thinking, we spray or step on some insects even though we would never consider hurting or killing a butterfly, which is nothing more than a metamorphosed "bug," or the end product of a crawling insect. Just think, if we changed our mindsets about insects, we would gain a whole new world of subjects to view and photograph!

The best time to photograph insects is during the cool of the morning when they are still sluggish from the damp, cool night air. Butterflies, for instance, have a tendency to spread their wings under the morning sun to warm their bodies and dry the dew on their wings.

Damselflies and dragonflies also dry off in the morning sun. They return to the same wetlands and perch, time after time. It is easiest to approach them when they are preoccupied during mating season or hunting mosquitoes. Quickly move in, set up your camera equipment and sit very still. They will return to their favorite perch, just feet from you.

Butterflies are best photographed in the early morning light when they are still and have their wings spread to dry from the damp of the night's mist.

You can find honeybees feeding on flower nectar as they move from plant to plant with the blooming of new buds. While some flying insects, such as moths, are active primarily at night, they can be viewed easily. Simply turn on a light, and they appear. Ants and yellow jackets will find you—just have a picnic.

Spiders are arachnids, not insects, and they range in size from microscopic species such as mites to large bird–eating spiders of tropical rain forests. Most spiders are not only harmless but also quite helpful because they keep insect populations in check. There are only two dangerous species in North America: the black widow and the brown recluse. Both are found throughout the southern part of the United States. Scorpions, not classified as spiders but close cousins, are found primarily found in the Southwest and Florida.

Spiders have a limited home range and are relatively easy to find and photograph. Find a web and you will find a spider. When searching for webs, look into the sun because light reflects off the strands. With the sun at your back, you will not see the webs because the light passes through them. Morning light has the greatest angle and bejewels webs with tiny dew drops. If there is no mist or dew on a web, use a mist sprayer filled with water.

When photographing a bejeweled spider web, try shooting into the sun at an angle. This backlighting allows the light to reflect through the droplets and accents details and outlines. By using a reflector or piece of cardboard, you can block the wind, for even the slightest breeze will cause the web to move and blur the image.

I find the best time to photograph spiders is when the mist and dew are heaviest.

A Geas spider web bejeweled by early morning mist was captured by shooting into the sun. W

Lyme's Disease

Lyme's disease is caused by a bacteria that is spread via infected deer ticks. An infected tick must break the skin before transmission of the bacteria can occur.

Deer ticks are easy to overlook because they are very small, about the size of a period on this page. Larger ticks are not known to carry Lyme's disease but may carry Rocky Mountain spotted fever. Although a deer tick's bite is painless, symptoms of the illness typically begin with a red, ring-shaped rash around a red, pin-sized bump.

You can pick up ticks in any wooded or grassy area. They can fall on you, but more often they grab onto your clothing as you brush by a plant or weed. Always check yourself and your clothing after being outside, even in your yard. If you know there are ticks in your area, tuck your pants into your socks, spray your shoes with tick repellent, and, most important, regularly check yourself and your children while outdoors and immediately upon going indoors. A good hot shower with soap and washcloth upon returning from the field not only feels great but also helps remove any ticks.

Working with amphibians and reptiles often means getting dirty and wet. W

Amphibians and Reptiles

"The frog does not drink up the pond in which he lives."
—Indian Proverb

Misunderstood and often mistreated, amphibians and reptiles are important members of temperate and tropical ecosystems. Commonly known as herps, they consume large numbers of insects and rodents that would otherwise overrun our planet.

All amphibians and reptiles are cold-blooded, or ectothermic, animals. Their body temperature is roughly the same as the environment they inhabit. They prefer places with warm, consistent temperatures. Herps native to cooler climates hibernate in winter.

Herps have different metabolic systems from those of warm-blooded animals. Their body temperature fluctuates with the environment, and they do not burn up food or energy to maintain certain metabolic processes. They do not have to maintain a consistent body heat as required by warm-blooded animals.

However, they do utilize both the heat of the sun and the cool of the shade. They sun themselves to speed up their metabolic processes, such as blood circulation and food digestion. They shade themselves to keep from overheating on warmer days.

Amphibians and reptiles that occupy geographic areas with varying degrees of temperature are active only during the warmer months of the year—late spring, summer and early fall. They spend the colder winter months hibernating below wetland muck or in dens deep below the earth's surface, where the temperature is above the freezing point.

You may find many reptile species in a desert valley but few in adjacent mountains. Your success rate of finding and photographing many types of herps will increase greatly the closer you get to the equator.

The best time of year for viewing and photographing herps in North America is in early spring when they are migrating to nesting and breeding areas. Also, cool sunny autumn days may entice them to come out into open areas to bask in the sun or soak up heat from baked sand or blacktop.

Here are a few tips on how to approach reptiles and amphibians:
- If an individual animal has not been handled or teased before, it may allow you to approach in daylight.
- Move extremely slowly and cautiously. Sudden movements will cause your subject to quickly disappear.
- Many herps are delicate creatures and should not be handled. If left in the sun or a hot car, overheating can be fatal quickly.
- Be patient and still. Wait for them to return to a favorite spot.

Because reptiles and amphibians are found most often on the ground, most people photograph them in documentary fashion—looking down at them. This method shows color, shape and size, but for nature art or the best possible photographic results and images that speak to the viewer, try to photograph subjects at eye level—frog to frog. This inevitably means kneeling or lying on the ground. Because so many different amphibians and reptiles live in wetlands, this means lying in mud, muck or water. Do not be afraid to get wet to capture an image. Be prepared for such opportunities:
- Wear hip boots, chest-high waders, or an old pair of sneakers. Wear old pants, and carry a change of clothing for your return trip. A piece of plastic or drop cloth will allow you to lie flat on the ground without getting wet and dirty. Be careful where you lie, not only

for your safety and comfort, but also so as not to harm organisms in whose habitat you are a guest. Caution: When you are "belly shooting" in the West, be alert for plants that have spines and spikes, even tiny hairlike ones. Rattlesnakes also rest in cool shaded areas. In the Midwest and East, chiggers (redbugs) and sand fleas can ruin your trip. They can infest your jacket if you put it down in the wrong spot. I have found that a bath in Tide detergent kills the pest and stops most itching.

● Carry a top viewfinder adapter for your camera, so you will not have to get extremely low to the ground. With a standard eyepiece view camera, you may have to dig a hole for your chin or lie on your side just to see through the viewfinder.

● Carry a small table-top tripod, which you can place on the ground or in shallow water at eye level to the subject. A tripod ensures stability when trying to photograph from an awkward position. Under adverse conditions, there is a tendency to move, shake or sway slightly, and these movements can wreck what should have been a perfectly good image. Craning your neck at strange angles to use a ground-level camera may result in crooked horizons and in disappointment when your images return. Use a tripod.

Frogs and toads

A favorite sound is the peep, peep, peep of spring peepers when they begin their mating calls. On warm, rainy spring evenings in the East, you can find hundreds of peepers crossing back roads near woodland swamps or wetland areas in search of mates.

Most frogs and toads lay their eggs in water. These eggs hatch into tadpoles and ultimately transform into adults. Peepers start their mating just as winter snows melt, and they are soon joined in the same wetland areas by mating frogs, toads and salamanders. Later in the season, wetlands are filled with mating green frogs, then bull frogs. Loud "jug-o-rums" can be heard in summer.

During courtship only the male frogs vocalize, announcing they are ready, willing and able to mate. Most of this vocal-

A lizard's vision is such that it only detects movement, so you have to be willing to sit and wait. W

ization occurs just before dark and continues until about midnight when temperatures drop.

Most amphibians are creatures of habit. If a frog jumps into the water from a particular lily pad, it often will return to the same pad once it feels it is safe to do so. When photographing frogs, try lying at the water's edge and waiting for them to return.

At night, I use a headlamp to free my hands and to be unencumbered while holding and focusing my camera. The light beam does not seem to bother frogs, but it tends to freeze them in place for a short time. Frog and toad calls are often tough to pinpoint, so triangulate with two light sources and look at the cross point.

Be cautious not to bother or alter frog behavior. They vocalize, protect territory, feed and mate only if unmolested. If you affect their behavior, they suffer. Research shows that frogs may be indicators of our planet's health. Frog numbers have decreased alarmingly, and scientists speculate the declines may have been caused by global warming, changes in the ozone, increased ultraviolet rays and other environmental alterations. Let's not challenge them even more.

Lizards

More so than most reptiles, many lizards have definite home ranges. When I discover a lizard, I sit motionless and observe what it is doing. Its actions often become predictable as it moves to the same observation points and favorite sunning spots.

Although most lizard species are predators, they are also prey and therefore extremely skittish. Like most prey species, lizards have keen senses and will spot you long before you see them. If you scare off a lizard, wait patiently for it to return.

Natural evolution has designed lizards with eyes on the sides of their head for a wide field of view. In the extreme case of old-world chameleons, the eyes work independently of each other, allowing them to see 360 degrees. Although lizards can see wide views, they can only perceive movement. If you remain motionless, lizards may not detect you. They will view you simply as part of the landscape.

Peepers and tree frogs are easiest to locate during nighttime hours. C

A long telephoto, coupled with a close-up adapter, will enable you to photograph small creatures from a distance. I photographed this colorful 4 inch Mauritius lizard from 25 feet. C

One simple method of capturing good lizard imagery is to set up a tripod at some point along the lizard's course of travel. Mount your camera and focus on a specific point along the lizard's route or favorite observation point. Then move back slightly and wait with a shutter release cord in hand. A long lens is necessary because their comfort/flight zone is large. A telephoto lens with extension tubes allows close focus. A reflector also works great to fill shadows and put a sparkle in their eyes.

Note: The Gila monster of the Southwest and the bearded lizard of Mexico are the only two poisonous lizards in the world. They are secretive, rare and protected by law.

Salamanders

As amphibians, salamanders differ in behavior from their reptilian lizard relatives. Salamanders prefer slightly cooler, damper, darker habitats than lizards, which prefer warm, dry and brightly lit

habitats. Lizards have leathery dry skin, are terrestrial egg layers, move fast and can be found in open areas. Salamanders have moist skin, are jelly–like and often lay aquatic eggs. You can find them hiding in darkened forest areas under rotting trees and logs and in streams.

Some species of salamanders, such as the spotted, breed before all ice melts during February, but most salamanders leave their woodland hibernation areas and seek lowland pools or other moist places for breeding during the late rainy spring. Salamanders prefer to migrate on warm rainy nights when moisture is high. The moisture lures them out of hibernation, and during a good downpour, hundreds sometimes can be found crossing country lanes and roads in woodlands.

The best time for photographing salamanders is during their spring migration, but some salamanders can be found in late summer and early fall. In the West, tiger salamanders are found

Most snakes are harmless, but it still helps to work with an assistant when photographing them. C

often in and around cattle tanks and other small ponds.

If you ever turn over a log or rock while looking for salamanders, put it back exactly as you found it. Their survival depends on you doing so. It takes a long time for a log to settle into place to create a perfect habitat for these and other secretive creatures.

Salamanders are even more delicate than lizards. When working with them, do not allow their skin to become dry. If you need to touch a salamander, be gentle and moisten your hands before picking it up. Dry fingers can be harmful to salamanders because their skin has a mucous coating that protects it from desiccation and infection.

The skin of a salamander placed in the sun will quickly dry out turn into a sticky paste that will adhere to anything it touches like flypaper. Use a mist bottle to keep the skin damp.

Although salamanders generally move slowly, they move deliberately and can move quickly out of your picture frame. Because they also prefer dark habitats, taking their pictures can be difficult.

As part of your general photographic equipment, carry a collapsible circle reflector and use it to illuminate the subject. The added reflective light allows you to see better and focus more easily without having to move the animal into brightly lighted areas. This type of added reflective light does not generate nearly the heat of a mechanical light and allows the subject to stay cool and moist.

Under these low–light conditions, use either very fast film or a fill flash to stop any potential movement and to bring out subtle colors in the decaying vegetation.

Snakes

Although often misunderstood and feared, most snakes are harmless and all are beneficial. In the United States there are only four major types of poisonous snakes: rattlers, copperheads, cottonmouths and coral. The first three are all members of the pit viper family. If a person is bitten, the snake's venom affects the individual's hemoglobin's ability to carry oxygen. The coral snake is in the cobra family, and its venom is a neurotoxin. Its poison affects the victim's nervous system.

Snakes often can be found in and around rock piles at the base of cliffs or slopes. Such areas offer shelter not only for snakes but for may other smaller creatures, a food source for the snakes.

Stone hedgerows in the more temperate regions, stacks of logs and almost any pile of loose debris are good places to find woodland snake species. Rat, pine and corn snakes often can be found near farms, fields and other areas where mice are plentiful. Look for garter snakes, which feed primarily on fish, amphibians, and worms, in moist areas near their prey. Closely related water snakes reside in tree roots along embankments of ponds, lakes, and rivers where they feed on frogs and small fish.

Since snakes are cold-blooded animals, they sometimes can be found along roadways that soak up heat during the day and radiate it back on cool evenings. On an extremely hot day, snakes may be found in basements, in crawl spaces, and under shaded rock outcroppings.

Turtles are endangered primarily because of loss of habitat. Should you come across a turtle laying eggs, do not disturb her, her eggs, or her young after they hatch. W

Rattlers, garter snakes and black rat snakes hibernate in communal dens and often emerge in larger numbers in spring. Most snakes, however, are solitary.

Many published snake photographs are taken under controlled conditions, because snakes are fast-moving animals and do their best to avoid humans. Snakes do not hang around to have their pictures taken. It is usually best to photograph them by working with a herpetologist who knows how to handle snakes. It helps to have an assistant when photographing snakes, especially the poisonous ones.

Caution: If cornered or taken by surprise, snakes instinctively will defend themselves and may strike. If you are bitten by a harmless species, wash the bite with soap to prevent possible infection.

Turtles

Seemingly slow and clumsy with their heavy shells and stumpy legs, turtles have carried themselves well since the days before dinosaurs. They are fascinating.

A scared box turtle will withdraw into its shell totally encapsulated—no head, legs or tail available for predators. When it feels safe, it will emerge slowly and deliberately and study its surroundings by sniffing and probing. Then, as soon as one foot touches the ground, it scoots off.

In early spring, when the water temperatures are cool, painted turtles and sliders line up on floating logs and on embankments of small islands in ponds and lakes to bask in the sun. When the weather gets hotter, you will find them sunning only during the early morning and afternoon. At midday they return to the cool water to avoid overheating.

Freshwater turtles are easy to locate in wetland areas. Watch for splashes and ripples in the vicinity of logs or other floating objects as you approach. Turtles have fantastic eyesight and will dive into the water long before you see them.

North America has numerous species of turtles and tortoises, but their populations have significantly declined over the past few decades primarily because of habitat loss. Turtles also lose a large percentage of their eggs and newly hatched young to raccoons, skunks and opossums. Both water and land turtles lay their eggs in the spring and early summer preferably in patches of soft sand or dirt. Should you come across a turtle laying eggs, do not disturb her or her eggs because she may abandon the nest without laying all of her eggs or may not cover them properly. The result would be a decreased number of hatchlings.

Turtles are sensitive to movement, so after locating one or more of them, settle down and get comfortable in an area that gives you good visual contact. Set up a blind, or sit very still and wait. Turtles almost always will climb out on the same log they left as you approached.

Prefocus your camera with telephoto lens on that spot and wait for them to return. Exposures may be tricky. The water may be dark or light depending on whether there is a reflecting sky or dark foliage overhead. You may want to read your meter off a nearby subject that appears neutral in color.

Some turtles, such as snappers and soft-shells, behave somewhat differently than other wetland turtle species and are not located easily. They spend most of their life underwater, rarely sun themselves and are usually not seen except when they raise their snout above the surface to take a breath of air or when they travel over land to lay their eggs during early spring.

Caution: Snapping turtles and large soft-shells have long necks and move fast enough to catch passing fish. If they feel threatened they may defend themselves by lunging forward and inflicting a bite. They are much faster than most people realize and have powerful jaws with a razor–sharp bill. A snapper can easily take a finger or two!

A turtle-to-turtle, eye-to-eye perspective creates an image that communicates. W

Birds

"When the bird and the book disagree, always believe the bird."
—Birdwatcher's proverb

It is estimated that during late summer North America has a resident bird population of nearly 20 billion comprised of more than 650 different species.

Birds help humans by consuming many insects, weed seeds and rodents. Birds are also an indicator species because of their sensitivity to environmental changes. In recent years, many bird species have suffered drastic declines because of habitat loss and toxic pollutants.

These majestic creatures of the air have fascinated mankind since the beginning of time. Crude paintings of birds appear on walls in caves where Stone Age people dwelled. With time, birds became a symbol of the gods and an image of power. Birdlike figures were worshiped in ancient cultures. Today, they are symbols of great nations and grace the pages of more books and magazines than any other wild creature.

We go bird–watching and photograph birds because there are so many kinds of birds and because they are highly visible and easy to locate, particularly during breeding and nesting seasons. Birds can be appreciated by everyone, even those who live in cities and urban areas and those who cannot leave their homes. It is no surprise that bird-watching and photography rank among the most popular outdoor activities.

The key to locating birds is to stop, look and listen. The simplest and easiest way to find birds is to visit an area that offers you extensive visibility and a productive habitat for bird species. Meadows, marshes, beachheads, hedgerows, edges of fields, streams, ponds and lakes offer all the bird necessities—food, water, and shelter. They also provide clear views, so they are exceptionally good starting places for novice bird-watchers.

The time of year is also important when considering where to locate birds. Take into consideration the bird's migration, nesting and breeding patterns and its preferred habitat and foods.

Bird sensitivity

Birds are most sensitive to distractions when they begin to lay eggs, incubate, and raise their young. Try to minimize and avoid contact with birds during this time of year. Make sure that when viewing or photographing your actions never force a mother bird to leave her young or not allow her to return to her nest. Baby birds that are forced to be left to natural elements of heat and cold for prolonged periods of time stand a good chance of dying from exposure or predation.

The most critical time in a young bird's life is just before it is ready to fledge. They appear to be large enough to fly, but they do not have the strength. The pressure applied by an approaching viewer or photographer may force a young bird to prematurely abandon its nest. It will instinctively try to fly, but it will only succeed in fluttering and flapping its wings as it falls to the ground. Sometimes you can put these screaming juveniles back in their nest, but it is best to make sure you do not disturb nest sites.

Parent birds also will squawk and give off distress calls to try to scare you or draw your attention away from their young. Sometimes the calls work, but they also signal every predator in the immediate area. Predators also will follow your tracks to nests.

Most animals raise their young in close proximity to a food source. Find an animal's food source and chances are you will find the animal. These juvenile Great-horned owls were hatched adjacent to an open field with small rodents. C

The mortality rate is high. Approximately 60 percent of the eggs and young never leave the nest. Some bird species have a second nesting later in the year, and sometimes these second nestings are more important factors for the longevity of a bird species. A nesting site must be in an area with a minimum number of predators and have limited accessibility. It also needs to be close to an abundant food source. In areas where predators are nonexistent, cover is not necessary. Seabirds nest in areas with limited predation, and their nests tend to be open and exposed.

Feeding time

Almost all bird feeding habits are closely tied to and influenced by the time of day, time of year, and type of weather. Most land birds do most of their feeding in the early morning and in the late afternoon.

During spring when young birds are hatching, parents deviate from their usual feeding schedules and often are out all day gathering food to feed themselves and their young. Most birds take a reprieve around noon during the heat of the day. While they rest, we eat lunch.

Weather can play a noticeable role in a bird's feeding pattern. You may notice there is an increase in feeding activity before and after winter storms when birds burn up more energy.

Woodland species

When photographing and viewing birds, never cut or break back the foliage that hides a nest and blocks your view. Keep the nest hidden and protected from predators. The vegetation also helps stabilize the environment by keeping the heat out and the cool air in and vice versa.

By observing and following an animal that is carrying nesting material, you can find its nest. Nests should always be viewed and photographed from a distance. C

When photographing birds in heavy cover, use lightweight nylon cord and tie back only the interfering pieces of vegetation. Also, use a long lens, at least a 400mm, to give you more working room and your subject a larger comfort zone. After all, you want the bird to exhibit natural behavior. Mount your camera to a tripod and focus on the bird, its nest, or perch, and wait for the action. If a particular species is commonly skittish, attach a remote shutter release cord to your camera and move back a reasonable distance. Wait with binoculars in one hand and release button under your thumb in the other hand. When departing, untie your string and check to see each piece of disturbed foliage has been returned to its original position.

Most of these techniques are applicable to a wide variety of species. By doing your homework, you can tailor your strategies to specific species.

Songbirds

Passerines, or songbirds, can be found in almost every habitat and are easily identifiable by their songs. Small birds may sing because they are happy, but mostly they sing because they are marking their territory.

A songbird will fly to a perch, sing its "keep out" warning to others of the same species, then move to the next perch, and sing again. Time and time again a bird will return to the same perch, sit at the same point, and sing the same song.

The peak times for observing nesting behavior in passerines is in spring and early summer. The male, which is often smaller and more brightly colored than the female, arrives first to select a nesting territory. He defends his territory by singing

The bald eagle represents our dreams of frontier America.. W

from perch to perch, staking his claim against other males of the same species.

If you wish to view and photograph passerines, start by quietly walking woodland roads and field edges during their migrations north. Study the terrain, look for rock outcroppings and fallen and rotted trees. Watch the details before the leaves start to sprout. Upon hearing a song, use binoculars or spotting scope to pick out the singer through the trees. By taking notes you will be able to return on another day when the trees are full of foliage and still be able to locate the bird.

As spring arrives, you may attract house wrens, sparrows, chickadees, tufted titmice, bluebirds, jays, cardinals and numerous other woodland passerine species to backyard feeders. Some species will even nest near feeders. Install birdhouses by the end of March, and you may entice a number of birds to stay nearby.

Raptors

Finding raptors, or birds of prey, and their nests is relatively easy in the open areas of the Midwest and West. When a raptor is soaring in the sky, scan treetops along creeks with binoculars for trees large and strong enough to hold a nest.

Most raptor nests are large and bulky, making them fairly easy to spot in the early spring before the leaves sprout. If you find a nest, check it carefully with binoculars to see if a bird is nesting. All raptor species stay low in their nests, making them difficult to see.

Hawks and owls breed during different seasons and sometimes use each other's old nests even though they are enemies. Some of the larger owls, such as the great horned, do not build their own nest but borrow others. They lay their eggs as early as January or February so their young will have fledged before eagle, hawk, or falcon nesting begins.

Waterfowl

Although species diversity is limited in urban parks, photographing waterfowl is much easier there than in wilderness areas. Resident park species have become habituated to humans and allow viewers

At first, learn about animals close to home in local parks.

and photographers to approach unnaturally close. Under such conditions, photography becomes easy with no special preparation required. But keep in mind that birds need to carry on their daily activities. Their needs are greater than your need to view and photograph them.

When photographing waterfowl in the wild, be alert and well hidden. Try using a portable blind early and late in the day when ducks and geese are active. Place the blind at the edge of the water so you can photograph or view their activity with the sun at your back or side. Sometimes it helps to set up a blind the night before and arrive before daybreak when the ducks and geese start arriving.

As with most wildlife subjects, try to photograph at eye level for strong images. Try to get action photos of waterfowl diving and dipping below the surface. Look for images of waterfowl with water droplets on their bills and feathers and of birds taking off and landing. When a duck or goose cranes its neck, it is nervous and probably getting ready to take off. Focus on that bird.

To photograph landings, watch for patterns, such as a common landing direction or a turn just above a certain tree. Focus on the potential landing point and wait for the next subject to land. With a little practice, you will be able to predict and make the necessary last–second changes. These points apply to all waterfowl.

Colonies and rookeries

Many seabirds and wading birds have a tendency to nest in large groups called colonies and rookeries. Each spring or summer they return to the same cliffs, perches, beaches, tundra and stands of trees to upgrade existing nests or to build new ones. They primarily nest in large numbers for safety reasons and because of limited habitat or lack of nearby food sources elsewhere.

Seabirds prefer nesting along rocky coastlines or on islands. They migrate from the open oceans to the cliffs in spring and construct nests that are often no more than a stack of gravel or a small pile of grass or dried seaweed. Natural predation

Colonies of sea birds are exciting places to observe and photograph. They also are very sensitive areas, so be careful when approaching and leaving them.

is usually low so there is no need to conceal and hide their nests. The distance between each bird is often no greater than the reach of an extended neck. With the sea so close at hand, parents have easy access to fresh fish for their young. Many species spend the rest of their lives at sea and return to land only to breed.

Birds that live in colonies or rookeries are the easiest of all species to locate because their traditional nesting sites are well documented. With a little research you can learn the best places and times for viewing and photographing them.

When approaching these sites, be careful not to frighten a single bird, for one spooked bird can panic the whole colony into flight. And watch where you step when approaching a colony of ground-nesting birds, for their eggs blend in exceedingly well with their surroundings.

The outer edges of a colony have a lesser nest density than the thickly settled center. Work these edges for a number of reasons: you have room to set up a portable blind; less time for the few birds to settle down; and an opportunity to isolate individuals to keep pictures simple and less confusing.

To photograph a concentration of birds, use an adapter, a 1.4 or 2X converter, and reach out a little farther. The images will capture a concentration of birds without any disturbance. Shoot at their level if possible. You also can prefocus successfully because you know exactly where they are going to land. Use a fast shutter speed and catch them hovering just above the nest about to touch down or transfer food to mates.

Photographing birds leaving a scene is relatively easy compared to capturing them as they approach. The secret is anticipating their next move.

Shorebirds

Your photographic schedule and the shorebirds' feeding schedule fluctuate with the tides. Shorebirds feed heaviest on the outgoing tide. Their choice foods are crustaceans and small plants and animals that are exposed along open mud flats and sandy beaches.

Shorebirds are always on the move while feeding. They peck here, then move there, peck again, and go from one spot to another, all in close proximity. While feeding, they are exceedingly hard to photograph because they never stand still long enough for you to focus. After checking the tide charts, arrive early and set up a blind at the edge of a beach or marsh. Locate the blind so that you will be able to photograph the birds moving into the frame, not out, and so you can have some empty, or negative, space ahead of the subject.

Most shorebirds nest in the tundra regions of the far north and sometimes in smaller, less homogeneous populations than seabirds. Their nests are often nothing more than scratches in the sand where they lay their tiny speckled eggs that blend in so well. Some birds, like oystercatchers, prefer nesting in reeds and grasses of back bay islands.

Wading birds

Like most fisherman, wading birds have preferred fishing spots and return to them daily. Through continuous observations, you will be able to identify these feeding spots. If you are a keen observer, you also may notice the same bird in the same spot at the same time of day. Once you become familiar with a bird's behavior, set up your portable blind a short distance away from its favorite fishing hole an hour or so before its projected arrival. If possible, stay in the blind until after the bird leaves.

Wading birds such as snowy egrets and great blue herons build small, treetop rookeries. These species congregate in an area with good cover and, more importantly, with poor predator accessibility. They construct nests of sticks in which to raise their young high above the ground. Other wading birds, such as the American

Setting up a blind before your subject arrives is the only way to capture certain species doing what they do naturally.

bittern and least bittern, are much more reclusive. It is difficult to find their nests in thickly reeded and grassy wetlands.

Backyard birds

Of all animals to entice into your backyard, birds are the easiest. All you need is an ample supply of food, water and shelter. Regardless of how much food you put out, most birds will not cross wide-open spaces. Instead, they will seek out food that is near shelter. Dense hedgerows and bushy plants such as multiflora rose, bayberry, autumn olive, and honeysuckle offer good shelter and an abundance of natural foods for most songbirds. Evergreens also provide good shelter and food.

To photograph birds around backyard feeders, the trick is to make the image look as if it were photographed in a more natural setting and that takes a little planning. Start by placing a feeder in an area where you will not be shooting into the sun. If possible place it at least five to ten

feet from dense cover. Between the feeder and cover, look for a natural perch, a tree with branches. Birds also will quickly use a pole with a small twig taped or stapled to its top. Place it a few feet from the feeder in the best position for your photography, and birds will stop there often before going to the feeder.

If you have a variety and many birds going to the feeder, they will use the modeling perch to wait their turn. Change the twig occasionally to add variety in your photos. Try to use a branch with which the species is most often associated.

As a bird approaches a feeder, it will often sit in nearby cover to make sure the coast is clear, then it will hop to a perch closer to the feeder. Before going in to pick a seed, it will scan the area for predators. After the bird has a seed, it will return to another perch to open and eat that seed. Note that a bird will continue to use the same perch. Before the bird has a seed and just after it has finished eating and dropped the shell are by far the best times to photograph.

Besides a feeder, another bird magnet is a small fountain or any trickle of water. Even a pan with a sloping rock in it will do. Small birds love a place to bathe. Strategically place a few more rocks to hide the pan or watering dish to create a more natural photograph. If you use a flash, you can freeze the bird's fluttering and catch water droplets as they shake and fly.

If you have an open backyard devoid of wildlife, it is easy to create a habitat that attracts an abundance of species. Before you plant any trees and shrubs, do a little research to find out what lives and grows naturally in your region and what specific birds prefer for cover and food. For quick and easy starters, you can always use potted plants to create cover and to provide perches. Move the potted plants around to change your photographs.

The more diverse you make your backyard habitat, the greater the diversity of species you will attract—and the greater the photographic and viewing opportunities!

Note: If you install a feeder in your yard and feed birds in the fall, be sure to continue feeding them throughout the winter and into late spring until natural food becomes available again.

Hummingbirds

Because hummingbirds dart and flutter from flower to flower in rapid succession, they are difficult to view and photograph.

Even the fast-moving hummingbird needs a perch to land on like this flower. Sometimes a perch placed near a hummingbird feeder may be just what is required. C

Birds Help Control Insects

Nature has evolved its own balanced system. Each bird species has a specific ecological niche or role in which the bird functions for survival.

Some birds search through trees and hop on the ground eating countless bugs, beetles, and grubs that would otherwise devastate forests and crops. Woodpeckers, for instance, help control bark beetles that can devastate wooded areas quickly. Seed-eating birds help keep down the prolific growth of undesirable weeds.

Most important to us are the birds that eat flying insects. Swallows, swifts, flycatchers, and others return to the same area each year just as the insects hatch and take to their wings and before a large percentage can lay more eggs. It is this system of checks and balances that keep areas from being inundated by hordes of destructive insects.

Birds have been greatly affected by humans. We have altered or destroyed natural habitats needed to sustain populations of many migratory birds and other wildlife. We poison our world with toxic pesticides and herbicides to keep insects and weeds under control. Many of these chemicals kill birds and other animals.

Did you know that one songbird can control as many or more insects as spray and poisonous chemicals? According to Gardening Without Poisons, a book by Beatrice Trum Hunter, a swallow will eat 1,000 leaf hoppers in 12 hours. A house wren will feed its young 500 spiders and caterpillars during one afternoon. A pair of flickers will consume 5,000 ants as a mere snack! A thrasher can eat more than 6,000 insects a day, and a purple martin will consume between 2,000 and 14,000 mosquitoes a day. These figures are just a few examples of how important birds are in controlling insect populations.

Centuries ago, Native Americans had to cope with similar or worse insect populations than we do today. They looked to nature to control nature. They hung hollow gourds throughout and around their encampments to entice birds to live with and among them. In turn, the birds kept the insect populations low.

Today, many people have lost touch with nature and do not realize that wildlife, especially birds, are of enormous importance to mankind. It is up to us to take better care of the habitats we share with the birds and all other wildlife.

Each flower has enough nectar to attract but not hold a hummingbird in one position for long.

One good way to photograph hummingbirds is to use a long-necked hummingbird feeder. Place the feeder in an area that has good lighting and photographic appeal and allow the birds to become accustomed to the feeder. Then, take a long-stemmed flower blossom and slip it over the feeder neck. Prefocus with the flower off to one side, allowing room for the bird in the image and being careful not to show the feeder. Move away from the feeder to give the hummers lots of room. With a long lens and a remote, release the shutter when the hummingbird returns to the feeder.

Position the feeder so the background is simple. Use a piece of colored material behind the feeder. Place a small twig for a perch a couple feet from the feeder. Hummingbirds, especially the territorial males, will use it constantly. A flash helps freeze the rapid movements of the hummingbird's wings.

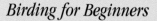

Birding for Beginners

Getting started in the fascinating and perhaps lifelong hobby of birding can cost less than a good dinner out. The most expensive piece of equipment you will need is a pair of binoculars. Although high-quality models with superior optic magnification and clarification can be costly, most basic binoculars can be purchased for as little as $30. In time, you may wish to invest in a spotting scope, which has a greater magnification than binoculars.

Next, you will need a bird identification book. Before you buy one, spend some time reviewing and comparing them. Look for field guides that cover the areas and species you are interested in. Contact your local Audubon Society chapter about outings to local parks, refuges, wooded lots, and other birding sites. These events will give you opportunities to try a variety of binoculars and to see which field guide other birders prefer.

Keep a record and count of all the different birds you identify. A small notebook is all you need. The list should reflect where you went, the species identified, the time of day it was spotted, the date, and weather conditions. From these notes you will be able to determine which species are most common during a particular time of year in different areas. Later, your trip lists can be converted into a life list, a master listing of all the bird species you have seen and identified. You can compare your list with a species checklist for your region provided by your local birding club.

To tell one bird from the next, train your eye to look for distinctive traits. First, note the bird's dominant color. Try to determine what colors appear on the bird's head, neck, wings, and tail. You may even be able to distinguish the colors of its beak, legs, and feet, which are helpful and important identification points, especially when identifying rare and seldom-seen species.

Next, look at its shape. Is the bird short or long, thin or fat? Is its head crested or smooth? Is its tail long or short? Is its beak curved or straight? These attributes are all distinguishing features of its silhouette and are used to determine a bird's family.

To distinguish species within the same family, look at the bird's markings. Are there stripes on its wings or tail? Does it have a ring around its eye or bill? These markings are often the only visible differences between subspecies.

When you watch a bird, look at how it flies. Its flight pattern alone can sometimes tell you what type of bird it is. Does it glide or move its wings fast or slow? Does it bob and weave or fly level? Many times behavioral traits are as important as any other identification characteristic.

Ultimately, as you learn more about birds, you will begin to recognize a particular species' song. This will allow you to identify a bird long before you see it. After a while you will start to recognize bird families and what type of birds to expect in what habitat.

Once you have mastered some of the basic birding techniques, you will be able to easily identify birds anywhere, anytime. At first the process of identifying birds seems involved, but it becomes second nature with practice.

Wildlife has no schedule to keep and no particular place to be at any particular time. Patience can greatly improve your viewing and photographing experience. But there is no substitute for being in the right place at the right time. C

Mammals

"For every creature we see, ten have already seen us and have hidden or moved away without our even being aware of it."
—Leonard Lee Rue, III

Of all creatures, land mammals sometimes are the hardest to find. They have evolved and survived because of their elusiveness and adaptive abilities. Mammals are everywhere, even in urban habitats. Rats, mice, raccoons, foxes, skunks and even coyotes reside in the heart of cities. They are all elusive species. They live not only in urban parks but in pipes, tunnels, basements, abandoned buildings and piles of trash during the day while people roam the streets. When the sun sets and we retreat into our homes, they come out of hiding to hunt each other and scavenge on our garbage.

The range and number of mammal species we can expect to find expands the farther we move from civilization. Otter, bear, elk, deer, bobcat and other species inhabit areas with the mice, rats, raccoons and skunks. To find truly wild creatures, we need to go where they reside.

Insect species are countless and everywhere. Amphibians and reptiles as a whole often have limited ranges, and many types are tied to wetlands. Birds flicker through the sky and are easily attracted to feeders. These animals are relatively easy to find in comparison to land mammals, which are often nocturnal, which blend in naturally with their surroundings and which roam for miles. They hide as they see, hear, or smell our presence. They make their homes underground, in dense forests, along mountain ridges, in swamps and in thickets. They are elusive and often reclusive. Predator or prey, they rely on wariness and stealth to survive.

To find any wild creature, you must know particular characteristics of a species and its habitat. The more you know about a city, the easier it is to find an address. Similarly, the more you know

Knowing where to look is an essential element in finding wildlife in urban settings. C

about an animal and its natural requirements and behavior, the easier it is to find the animal. Does it have a specific territory or home range? Dall sheep, for instance, are found only in the mountainous ranges of Alaska; caribou in the northern tundra; sea otter in western coastal waters; mountain goats on jagged rocky slopes in the Northwest.

What time of year are they commonly found in a given area? Deer, for example, feed on the lowlands during winter and at higher elevations during summer. Are they influenced by migration and breeding patterns? Caribou have traditional summer breeding grounds. What and when do they eat? Bison eat grasses and if left undisturbed feed early and late in the day. Where can they find the most abundant food source? Foxes live in areas with high rodent populations. How close are their water sources to their food sources, what are their shelter requirements?

These grizzly bear tracks tell us a bear has passed, even if you never actually see one. W

By answering such questions we can learn where to find mammals. We can gain most of that knowledge from books at home and can put it to work when we go out in the field. That is when we become detectives collecting evidence and applying motives and behavioral patterns. Rather than just hoping to see a certain species, we are solving a mystery, and we do not want to scare away our quarry while we are picking up its physical signs and clues.

Finding and interpreting wildlife signs in the field is much harder than the book research primarily because we have undeveloped skills. It takes a lot of time, practice and patience to become skillful at reading physical signs and clues. Even then, mammal sightings are not guaranteed, but you can still enjoy being a wildlife detective.

Tracks

In locating deer, for example, look for tracks and browsed vegetation. Tracks are the easiest of all wildlife signs to find, identify, and follow. With good tracks there is no mistaking an animal's identity. Gender cannot always be determined by tracks, but size of the tracks gives us a clue whether, for example, it is a buck or a doe, and the size might tell us whether it is a fawn. Tracks tell us where an animal is going and where it has been. Has it left the field, and is it heading to the stream? Tracks can also tell us whether the animal was walking or running. Long deep scuffs with penetrating toes portray running; more uniform, clean, sharp tracks imply walking. Tracks tell us about how long ago the animal passed by. If the edges look soft, a fair amount of time has passed.

Scats

Identifying scats is much less of a science than tracks but an important clue in identifying animals and their presence, especially when no tracks are evident. Droppings are distinctive in size, shape, and color and are fairly easy to identify.

Plant eaters, or herbivores, leave scats that tend to be small and uniform in texture. Scats of meat eaters, or carnivores,

Many animals mark their territory in different ways. This black bear is leaving claw marks in the tree to announce its presence to other bears. C

and those eating both plants and meat, or omnivores, tend to be larger and nonconforming in shape and contain seeds, bones, fish scales, and hair particulates. Scats tell us what an animal has been feeding on, and finding the food source may help us find the animal.

Coyote droppings are easy to spot in some areas, because coyotes do not take much care to hide them. Bobcats on the other hand are very meticulous, and you will rarely see their scats. Owl "pellets" of regurgitated undigestible bones and hair are easy to find and give away an owl's favorite tree. You can even identify the species of mouse eaten by the skull found in the pellet.

Environmental disturbances

Other clues to look for include disturbances to the environment, particularly vegetation. These clues range from the slight nibbling of grass and nipping of buds to heavily traveled trails and large dams across streams. Such environmental disturbances tell us something about what an animal eats, how it travels, and where it lives.

Some signs, such as prairie dog and gopher mounds and beaver and muskrat lodges, are obvious to even the untrained eye. But most wildlife signs are subtle, such as the matting or parting of vegetation and grasses for trails, beds, runways, rolling places and tunnels.

A large number of mammals are herbivorous that depend on the consumption of plant material for survival. Cottontails and deer browse on plants and twigs, but they each have a different biting pattern. Deer browse not only on the ground but also up to about four feet. They even will stand on hind legs to reach succulent growth. Porcupines, on the other hand, forage on the upper portions of tree trunks. They chew off the bark and consume it while sitting on a branch.

Bark scrapings may be caused by a deer rubbing its antlers to remove velvet for the fall rut or by a black bear sharpening its claws. Some animals also leave scrapings to advertise their presence to other animals. Small scratches on a tree may indicate climbing by an animal, and signs of digging and scraping of the earth may have been made by mammals foraging for insects, bulbs, and tubers.

As you spend more time in the outdoors and more time reading about mammals, you will be able to identify what animals live in an area by their tracks, scats, dens, burrows, tunnels, bark scrapings, nips and nibbles.

Nests and lodges

The collection and arrangement of vegetation into an orderly pile usually signifies the shelter or lodge of a wild creature. A gathering of leaves in a tree may be the home of a squirrel or deer mouse. At ground level, such a home may harbor voles or cottontail rabbits. In the water, a dam and a lodge of sticks may represent a beaver's residence and a lodge of reeds, a muskrat's home.

Cavities

Mammals may or may not create cavities, but they certainly use them as homes and shelters. Some cavities, such as rock crevices, hollow logs, and upturned stumps, are natural in origin. Some, like woodpecker holes and hollowed out areas under fallen logs, are made by animals. And wild animals use manmade cavities such as street culverts, chimneys,

A common visitor to many suburban backyards is the white-tailed deer, its grazing patterns are as easily recognized as its footprints. W

house eaves, and spaces under porches. It is often difficult to know what animals may be using these cavities unless you actually see them or can identify other nearby signs, such as food remains, hair follicles, scats and tracks.

Tree cavities especially are important to many forms of wildlife from bees and birds to small mammals and bears. That is why landowners are encouraged to leave some dead trees standing instead of turning them all into firewood.

Food remains/stores

Signs of animals feeding are strong indications that creatures live nearby. Food remains also can tell us what animals live in a given area. A stripped pine cone says a red squirrel or chipmunk may be at work. Chewed nuts may mean a gray squirrel or mouse. Nibbled mushrooms are often the work of a vole, mouse or squirrel.

Piles of grasses in a mountain rock cavity may represent the storage work of a pika. Stockpiles of nuts in a hollowed log could only mean a mouse or squirrel plans to feed on them throughout the winter months. Piles of branches in a wetland indicate a beaver's winter stash.

Scattered feathers are often the workings of a fox or hawk. Fish scales on an embankment were likely left by an otter. Freshwater clam shells on the shore are telltale signs of raccoons. A mule deer carcass chewed apart in a western wilderness area may be the doings of a cougar. The remains of a full-grown moose or caribou may indicate a culling by a pack of wolves or a grizzly bear.

Finding all the proper signs greatly increases the likelihood you will encounter the animal you seek but does not guarantee it. You may conclude a beaver lives in a particular area, because you have seen fresh stumps, a flooded area behind a stick-and-mud dam, and a lodge of sticks and mud piled up in the middle of a flooded area, but the beaver may have picked up your clues and gone into hiding.

This river otter has made its home under an abandoned boathouse near the water's edge.C

*A long lens lets you stay out of sight and smell when photographing in the wild.*C

Unless you stumble upon their tracks in the snow or upon the remains of a fresh kill, you may never know of the presence of such elusive mammals as foxes, wolves, cougars, lynx, badgers and wolverines.

Besides knowing wildlife signs and clues, an understanding of a mammal's behavioral patterns and motives can help us better predict where the animal is and what it might do next. And an educated prediction increases our ability to see and photograph the mammal.

Of the 4,000 or so mammal species worldwide, only a small percentage have been studied thoroughly. Most mammalian lives remain a mystery to both scientists and nature lovers even though they, too, are mammals. We humans have lost or sup-pressed many of our senses, so we should not apply our motives and behavioral patterns to other mammals. We must learn their motives and behavioral patterns.

Home range

Most mammals tend to stay within a given area or home range and create certain trails over time. They often mark their home range with scents to denote their presence to potential mates and rivals.

By sitting in a blind near a well-worn wildlife trail, you may be rewarded. Sometimes you sit for days and see nothing. Sometimes you have many wildlife sightings in short periods.

The size of home ranges varies greatly within and among species. Predators and

Many predators, like this mountain lion, have a wide range. Many photographers prefer to use wild-life models rather than put excessive stress on these reclusive mammals. C

scavengers, primarily meat eaters, tend to have large home ranges. They are higher up the food pyramid, and their food is more dispersed. Large mammals have large home ranges because of their need for greater quantities of food and because of the ease in which they can travel great distances. Small mammals tend to have small ranges. Some species migrate short distances or long distances between summer and winter ranges.

The major determining factor in the size of an animal's home range is the availability and abundance of food. If there is a large quantity of food in a given area, the range is small; a small amount of food, and the range is large. Another factor contributing to the size of a home range is the repro-

ductive cycle. When looking for a mate, many mammals expand their ranges.

Some home ranges overlap. Male sheep and deer often share the same home range during spring and winter until mating season, when males stake claim to a harem in a particular territory—an area that is actively defended against an intruder, usually of the same species. Males of many mammal species, such as cats, have home ranges that may overlap with females but not with other males. Many North American mammals do not have home ranges that are actively defended; rather, neighboring individuals manage to avoid each other's presence. Scent marks, rubs and scrapes clearly mark the borders, so encounters need not be physical.

These mountain sheep rams have chosen a rocky slope on which to bed down for the night safe from predators. If I had returned just before daybreak, chances are I would have caught them rising for a new day. W

Feeding

Each animal has evolved with a different need for food and a different strategy for acquiring it. Regardless of the technique of harvest or type of food, feeding is a primary mammal activity. This is true for herbivores, such as deer and goats; carnivores, such as mountain lions and wolves; and omnivores, such as grizzly bears and humans.

Plant eaters need plants and meat eaters need plant eaters. To find a particular mammal, you need to be where its food source is abundant and be there at a feeding time. Most mammals feed late in the day and throughout the night into early morning. They rest during the day. To see and photograph mammals, you need to be in the field before or as the sun rises or at their feeding site late in the day or early evening.

Seasonal changes

Animal behavior changes with the season and the availability of food sources. Herbivores such as deer, goats and rabbits have to adapt to the lack of green plant life with the coming of winter and shift to eating more bark and buds of trees and shrubs. Beavers, squirrels and mice survive the winter on their storehouses of large quantities of branches, nuts, and seeds respectively. Find a stash, and you may find a critter. But do not disturb these caches, for lives depend on them.

Another adaptation practiced by such mammals as woodchucks, marmots, bears, raccoons, skunks and opossums is to build up a fatty body layer to be used when food sources get low. These species gorge themselves on the plentiful food of summer and fall in building up their surpluses for the coming months. Some of these and other mammals get through the winter by becoming less active and therefore requiring less food. Raccoons, chipmunks, bears and woodchucks become less active and may sleep, or hibernate, for days, weeks or months in their well-protected dens. Interestingly, however, carni-

Some animals are best viewed and photographed at different times of the year. This muskrat or marsh rabbit is easiest to view and photograph with wetland vegetation at its thinnest–late fall, winter and early spring. W

vores stay active year round. This may be because their food source is not significantly changed with the seasons and because they scavenge on carrion.

Late summer and fall is a great time to observe and photograph mammals. Bull moose, caribou, elk and deer display magnificent antlers; bears have bulked up with a fatty layer for winter; red foxes and showshoe hares have thick winter coats. At this time of year their hair shines and glistens in the sunlight. This is also the time that hoofed mammals put on their displays of dominance in which they protect territories and actively pursue mates.

Be sure, however, that you are visible and alert to hunters and that you do not interfere with any animal's food gathering and feeding activities. A long hard winter decreases most mammal populations and may force some species to travel great distances in search of food and shelter. Nature weeds out the weak with falling snow. Only the strongest and fittest make

it through until spring to pass on their genes to another generation.

Spring is the start of new beginnings and a time to see and photograph most baby animals. This is also the time when females with young offspring are the most aggressive and instinctively do whatever it takes to protect them. Baby animals, especially mammals, are cute and photogenic. They are also curious but have not learned the dangers of approaching a person.

Mothers do a good job of hiding them, but young mammals, like most inexperienced youngsters, sometimes venture into unsafe areas. They may leave their dens to sun themselves and then venture a little farther. This is a good time to photograph young mammals—while they are active, inquisitive and not yet afraid of humans.

If you find a mammal den, try placing a blind some distance from the entrance. Then, over the course of weeks, move the blind a little closer each day. Too close too soon may scare the animals away, but when the blind and your scent gradually become part of their everyday lives, you can move the blind close enough to get good photographs with a telephoto lens of young playing outside the entrance. This type of photography requires a dedication of much time and a commitment to low/no impact on the animals' daily routine.

When entering or leaving the blind, be extra careful not to be seen by the animals. If they are truly aware of your presence, as opposed to your scent, the mother may move her young to another den.

Summer is the time when most, mammals can enjoy plentiful food and cover. As the young grow and are weaned, they learn to forage and survive. Last season's yearlings set out in search of their own territories.

Even though the temptation is great, never touch or allow the young of any wild mammal to touch you. Your scent will remain on them, and they may be abandoned by their mother. Never assume a young mammal, or any young animal, is abandoned or orphaned. A parent may be nervously watching and waiting for you to leave.

Scent markings

Most mammals have an extremely acute sense of smell. Scents help mammals locate food, mark territories and communicate with each other. Mammal scent markings are like road signs saying who lives nearby, who has passed through, and where food and water are located.

Mammals are constantly marking their world with scents, often in urine or scat but also by rubbing any of several scent glands on objects they pass. A dog does not urinate on every tree, bush or fire hydrant because it has to go but because it is marking a territory and telling other dogs he was there. You may think a cat is showing affection when it rubs its head and neck against your pants. Maybe it is, but it is also marking you with its scent.

Scents change with the season and situation and for a variety of reasons. Mammals mark their home, food and the areas in which they live. Their emotional

As a rule, predator animals will flee long before you ever have an opportunity to see or photograph them. C

Natural camou-flage has a way of protecting nature's young. If you are lucky enough to stumble upon a young animal, never touch it, because the mother may abandon it. C

state and reproductive cycles also change their scent and broadcast different messages from "keep out" to "come on in if you're of the opposite sex."

Mammals regularly mark and re-mark their claims to a home and a territory. I will leave it up to you to decide whether it is fortunate that humans cannot pick up most of these scents.

Reproductive behavior

One of the most motivating factors in all wildlife is the need to reproduce. From a species viewpoint, individuals live simply to reproduce another generation of offspring. Breeding wildlife populations are not always monogamous and those that are not may have more females than males and a single dominate male may sire

young from any number of females. Nature's objective is to ensure a next generation of stronger, fitter and environmentally better adaptive creatures. In the language of evolution and natural selection, "fit" means best adapted to survival and reproduction. Surplus males wander solo or form bachelor herds in some species.

Throughout most of the year, many mammals remain separated by gender and are reproductively inactive. Biologists believe the breeding cycle is probably triggered by the changes in photoperiod, the relative lengths of daylight and darkness. As mating season begins, the first priority is to locate a partner. This is done through scent and sound or a combination of the two. When reproductive time begins, females give off special scents excreted in

A bobcat responds to a free meal of fresh grouse, a sight you would not likely see in the wild C

their urine and feces or from glands.

During breeding season, both males and females become more active and may travel long distances in search of a mate. Males may become aggressive and can be vocal as they search for and protect their mate(s). They also may actively protect their territory from other males to reserve the sole right to breed with all females within the area; that insures that only their genes pass to the next generation. A male grizzly bear may even kill the young produced by another male and then breed with the female.

In some ways wild mammals are a lot like us, or we are a lot like them. When in love, some people travel to the ends of the Earth just to be together for a short time. Other mammals also will travel great distances to mate. Some species have been known to fight to the death over a mate or a mating territory.

Mammals have traditional mating rituals. Some rituals are quick and simple, others are long and complicated. Either way the animals often pay little or no attention to anything except their mate or mates. Though mating periods might be a great time for viewing and photographing, exercise caution, for the males can be very aggressive and dangerous.

After mating, most mammals return to their separate lives, perhaps so the female does not have to compete for limited food.

Looking and listening

Wild animals rarely stand like billboards announcing their presences. Often we catch only a glimpse of animals. Try and notice things that look out of place, things that do not quite fit in with their surroundings: a bump, an odd shape, a color that is too even or off a shade, a glistening of an eye, a twitch of a tail, a sheen of an antler, horizontal lines of belly or back, a rippling of water.

Listening for animals can be as helpful in finding them as reading all their signs and clues. If we listen to the sounds and noises of nature, we discover they can guide us in the general direction of wild creatures. Try sitting quietly in the middle

If you sit still long enough, some animals like these Dall lambs and ewes may wander over to visit, but first they will make sure you are not a predator. W

of a forest listening to every sound. When you hear the rustling of the leaves off in the distance, slowly turn your head in that direction. Do not move fast or move your whole body, only your head and do that slowly as if in a time lapse. Move your eyes and look in the direction from which the sound is coming.

At first you may not see anything. Sit and watch patiently. Allow your eyes to become acquainted with every leaf, twig, stick, rock, shrub and tree, and start to pick out differences. You may see or hear a flickering of leaves created by a chipmunk foraging for fallen acorns or the switching of a deer's tail brushing off summer flies. Subtle sounds often provide the first clues in detecting wildlife. Some sounds are more defined, such as the bugling of an elk during mating season or the snorting of a white-tailed deer when it has picked up a person's scent. The yelp of a coyote and the howl of a wolf are distinct and unmistakable sounds of the wild.

The game of naturalist Jeopardy gives us plenty of answers to questions about finding wild creatures. If we take the time to look for signs and clues, we will see that all kinds of mammals live around us in our cities and in towns as well as in our parks and wilderness areas. Animals live in every known habitat and can be found if we take the time to look for evidence.

Animal attacks

A number of people are attacked and hurt by wild animals in parks and refuges each year. This is unfortunate because most of the attacks are by animals that would not bother people under normal conditions and circumstances. It is our perception of wildlife that most often gets us into trouble. Wildlife found in a park or refuge is wild. Wildlife management areas are habitats protected for their intrinsic natural values and inhabitants. These areas are not zoos, and the creatures that reside there are not trained animals.

Our understanding of animals is different from an animal's understanding of humans. An animal's perception of being cornered or threatened often is different than ours. We must separate fact from fiction. While wildlife columns and documentary nature programs provide good information, many commercial films and publications are in the business of selling sensationalism, not reality. More often than not they portray wildlife as either cute and cuddly or ravenous and ferocious to depict a story line—man's story line, not nature's.

Nature's story can be found in quality textbooks, scientific journals, nature magazines and wildlife society publications and documentaries. They customarily provide accurate information that could save your life. All wild animals are potentially dangerous. With that in mind, here are some basic safety precautions to follow when you are trying to observe and photograph wild animals:

- When approaching an animal, always plan an escape route.
- Always leave the animal an escape route.
- Never put yourself between an adult and its young.
- Never approach to a point where you feel uncomfortable.
- Never sneak up or approach from a blind side.
- Never feed or attempt to feed a wild animal.
- Always look for wildlife's nervous and warning signs and stop and back off at the first indication of such signs.

If you are threatened by an animal or are attacked:

- Never run.
- Stand your ground and face the charging animal.
- Avoid eye contact with canine and bear species; eye contact may be perceived as a challenge.
- Establish eye contact with feline species to strengthen your position.
- Make loud noises, hold your equipment and arms up and out to make yourself appear larger than you are.
- Slowly back away, but never turn your back to the animal.

If you are attacked by a large carnivore, such as a bear, play dead and cover your stomach by pulling up your legs and cover your face and neck with your arms.

I am not sure I could play dead if I were attacked by a grizzly bear, but that is what the experts say could save our lives. The most effective strategy to avoid encounters is to give bears a warning. Let them know you are coming and they will likely step off the trail so you are not even aware of their presence. A bell on your shoes or on your walking stick, a soda can with a couple of pennies to rattle occasionally, even your best or worst rendition of "America the Beautiful" will warn them of your approach.

Utilizing Wildlife Models

Close-up portraits of wild animals have been made since the beginning of outdoor photography by using restrained or model animals. I would guess that 95 percent of published cougar photographs were done with restrained animals. You can tell the photographs from the wild by the cats' pinned–back ears after being run up a tree by a pack of dogs.

Keeping the animal's welfare in mind, the use of restrained and model animals has its positive points. Close-ups and portraits usually cannot and often should not be attempted in the wild. The close proximity necessary for such views places a wild animal at great stress, and most such opportunities just do not happen. A wild cougar will not run directly at you, let alone when you are prepared and have the camera ready. But an image of a trained cougar running at full speed toward the camera with every muscle rippling and staring intensely at the viewer as if it were prey is a valid image evoking every instinct of the wild animal. Persons opposed to any use of restrained animals for photography say that no valid behavior is depicted by restrained animals. Does a trained cougar run differently than a wild animal? I think not.

The important issue is the welfare of the restrained animals. I would never advocate catching wild animals for the specific use of photography. Granted, some of the animals available for photography have come from wild ancestors caught for this purpose. Most of the animals I am familiar with are several generations from the wild and are representative of that wild population. The care of these animals must be of highest quality, but even this standard does not satisfy some people. I would prefer to photograph all animals in a free state, but in today's world that just is not possible.

I hope that any photographer using restrained animals would label his or photographs with information to that effect. It is then up to the end user whether the photograph is appropriate for a specific use. Whether the publisher states that the image is of a restrained animal is seldom the decision of the photographer.

It is strange that nearly all of the widely published photographers, both still and motion, have used restrained animals all along but have kept it very quiet. Do the purists out there realize that Marty Stauffer, Jeff Foote, John Shaw, Carl Sams III, Perry Conway, Galen Rowell, Leonard Lee Rue III, Walt Disney, and Marlin Perkins have used restrained animals extensively? I find myself in good company, except that I seem to be one of the few to face up to the purists.

George D. Lepp
Freelance Photographer/Writer

Left: If you follow the call of the wild long enough, you may be lucky enough to capture it on film. C

Controlled Settings Are Unethical

Photographing controlled animals in game farm rent-an-animal situations is unethical in my opinion, because it is morally wrong and photographically incorrect.

I believe all creatures who inhabit the Earth and all elements of the Earth are related and beneficial to one another. Loving and respecting other creatures requires that I honor their needs to the same degree as I honor my needs. I cannot accept justifications for caging animals for use in controlled photographic sessions. I do not feel that as Homo sapiens we have the right to require other species to live in cages for the selfish or commercial use by humans.

Because I love and respect nature and all it gives us, I wish to photograph all elements of the Earth and my fellow creatures in the wild the way I find them. By documenting multiple aspects of our natural world as events happen in the wild, I feel good about my wilderness experiences and the resulting images. My wilderness photography enables me to go beyond simple illustration of nature subjects and into the realm of photojournalism.

Images taken in controlled situations are not representative of wild animals. Their wild nature has been removed in the process of training them to perform for their handlers. The setup conditions often do not replicate a wilderness situation. The animals are manipulated to act in ways that are contrary to their wild behavior. Furthermore, the animals are not free.

An ethical photojournalist reporting the news would never set up any type of situation for the purposes of a photographic session. Why should a nature photographer set up an animal shot and call it wild or even a wild setting? Is it ethical? Is it good photojournalism? I do not believe it is either.

We must be wilderness photojournalists if our work is to be respected by the masses. We need to be more than photo illustrators if we are going to show the wild nature of our natural world to the public.

Helen Longest-Slaughter
Natural History Photojournalist

Specifics for Bear Encounters

If a grizzly bear is encountered during a wildlife activity, your actions can affect the outcome. Maintaining a safe distance and manner that does not threaten the bear provides options for both you and it. A "cool" head is necessary to avert harm to yourself or the unnecessary killing of a grizzly bear.

If you encounter a grizzly bear, your first option should be to back out of the situation. Keep calm, avoid direct eye contact, back up slowly, and speak in a soft monotone. Never turn your back on a bear.

Never run. Do not climb a tree unless you have time to climb at least 10 feet before the bear reaches you. Remember, bears can run very fast—up to 35 miles per hour!

If the bear charges, stand your ground. Bears often "mock charge" or run past you. Shooting a bear when it is charging is not recommended. The bear almost always lives long enough to maul the shooter severely.

As a last resort, play dead. Roll into a ball, covering your neck and head with your hands and arms. Stay in a tucked position until you are sure the bear is gone. Many people have survived bear attacks using this tactic.

Interagency Grizzly Bear Committee
Forest Service
U.S. Department of Agriculture

Above: Some people never get the message—and some will never live long enough to get the message. In the wild, the next image would be a mauled man. C

This picture frame of coral polyps is no bigger than your smallest finger nail., and a single touch could crush dozens of unseen animals. By learning good diving skills, you become not only a safer but also an environmentally friendly diver. W

The Underwater World

"Sometimes we are lucky enough to know that our lives have been changed, to discard the old, embrace the new and run headlong down an immutable course. It happened to me on that summer's day, when my eyes were opened by the sea."

—Jacques-Yves Cousteau

A world within our world. A world of water. A world of perpetual motion. A world of mountains, valleys and trenches. A world often devoid of light, yet filled with vivid colors. A world prolific with life beyond any other. A world that we still know little about and a world we have only begun to discover.

More than two-thirds of our planet is covered with the magical element of water. Consisting of two hydrogen atoms and one oxygen atom, H_2O is a molecule all living things on our planet require for survival. It can be a solid, liquid or gas. It evaporates from the planet's surface, forms clouds, falls as rain, fills ponds and lakes, then flows as streams and rivers, and fills the oceans, only to repeat the process over and over again.

The makeup of water is such that we need to wear bales or weights to submerge ourselves in it and, in its cold temperatures, to wear exposure suits. Particulates suspended in the water limit our visibility, and at times they make our imaginations run wild as we wonder what might be lurking only a few feet away.

Our wonderful underwater world is still much a mystery. It was unknown to man until about 50 years ago, when a single key necessary for its exploration was developed, the self-contained underwater breathing apparatus. This invention unlocked the door to our marine environment. The key given to us by Jacques Cousteau is known today as scuba.

The pleasures of exploring and enjoying our underwater world do not come without their limitations. First, we must go through basic scuba diving training and be granted an open water diving certifica-tion. This permits us to begin to learn. Second, we are limited by the amount of time we can spend underwater, a period that varies relative to depth. Third, we are limited to the depths we can descend and to the rate at which we can ascend. Even with all these limitations there are few pleasures more enjoyable than to float through an underwater world teeming with marine life.

Snorkeling and diving on reefs

Do snorkelers and divers hurt reefs? Yes. We are unknowingly damaging and destroying reefs. On an average one-hour snorkel trip, an untrained snorkeler may touch a reef 50 times. An average diver may touch the reef 14 times. To the corals, sea fans and sponges that adds up to a lot of wear and tear.

Many divers also allow their equipment to drag across reefs often damaging marine life. Sometimes the equipment gets caught in nooks and crannies and causes additional damage— endangering the divers as well. Divers must be extremely careful not to become environmental hazards.

One of the hardest and most important tasks to master for comfort, safety and ecological protection is buoyancy control. If our buoyancy is incorrect, we struggle and spend our time underwater working at trying to become comfortable instead of enjoying the dive.

When using a new wet or dry suit, buoyancy control device (BCD), or new housing for a camera system or strobe, check your buoyancy, because it changes with different equipment. When properly buoyed, a diver with all air out of his BCD should float vertically on the surface with his eyes at the surface level. When testing to find out how much weight you need for proper buoyancy do so with all your gear, including underwater camera systems and strobes. Each piece of equipment changes your buoyancy.

No matter how many dives you have made, do a quick pool check of your equipment if you have not gone diving for a few months. Put fresh batteries in dive lights and dive computers to ensure they will not go dead when you are underwater. Check all clips, attachment rings, bells and whistles to make sure they are in working order.

When you go diving, properly anchor your boat, because an anchor can do much damage to marine organisms in a reef. Many popular and well-used dive sites have buoys to mark the sites and moorings. Some sites have submerged tie-offs, so a diver has to secure the boat. If you are in doubt about any permitted tie-off point, set your anchor in the sand adjacent to the reef.

Upon entering the water but before descending, give yourself a quick check to make sure everything is in working order and your gauge console, dive computer, dive light and any other equipment are properly attached.

Having mastered buoyancy control and having no dangling gear, you are ready to approach the reef. Good buoyancy control allows you to position yourself anywhere in the water column with only the slightest movement up and down with each breath. This is a beneficial and pleasurable technique for vertical wall diving and to get a closer look at small reef critters without causing damage to their home.

When approaching and leaving a reef, swim horizontally over a sandy bottom and try to stay just high enough off the bottom so the water pushed by your fins does not kick up sand and sediment. A

Our prolific underwater world is known to few first-hand. W

small amount of silt can suffocate corals and other marine organisms, and a lot of particulates can do even greater damage.

When visiting horizontal reefs, try to position yourself on a diagonal with your head facing downward. This enables you to look at all the small reef creatures, study coral formations, plan photographic strategies, focus cameras, position strobes and take photographs without fearing that a fin or knee might hit the reef. Such a position takes a little time getting used to. On walls or vertical drop-offs, position your body more or less horizontally, perpendicular to the reef face with your head up.

Try to use these horizontal and vertical reef-viewing techniques when looking for tiny creatures and for photographing. For general touring or an overview of an area, try to apply the same style and judgment that you might use when approaching and leaving a reef over a sandy bottom.

Before trying to navigate your way though a natural reef arch, first assess whether the arch is large enough to allow you through. Keep in mind that all your equipment nearly doubles your width. Even experienced divers forget how wide they are with all their gear and how long they are with their fins. To avoid kicking up sediment with your fins, change the traditional up and down kick cycle to a gentle sideways frog-kick. Then, as you swim through the arch, avoid exhaling. Air bubbles look wonderful trapped on the underside of a reef, but they will drown marine creatures in air.

Try not to touch a reef even with a finger. A single fingertip can crush a dozen coral polyps or crinoid tentacles. Although dive gloves will protect your hands from being cut and from being stung by hidden reef creatures like fire coral and hydroids, they were designed primarily to keep your hands warm and to protect them when gripping a line while descending, ascending and decompressing. Dive gloves were not made so you could hold onto a reef or grab marine creatures!

Marine animals

All marine creatures are intriguing. Some of them do not even look like animals. Some marine animals look like plants, and some marine plants look like slime. They come in strange shapes and forms, odd sizes and configurations. They are brightly colored or dull. Some have a

A coral reef is a living, breathing, reproducing organism, teeming with life. W

People often do not take the time to look for small things, but in the underwater world, it is the small things like this Christmas Tree Worm (1/2" tall) that give photographers their greatest pleasures. W

single color, and others come in a multitude of colors. Marine creatures come in seemingly endless variations.

The aquatic world is filled with blues and greens, but at times it can appear muted and monochrome. As we go deeper, it gradually becomes darker to a point of total blackness. The colors within the light spectrum dissipate as light travels through water. The first color of the spectrum to fade and disappear is red. At a depth of eight feet, red light starts to fade and is filtered out of the spectrum by 15 feet. The next diminishing color is orange at 15 feet; by 50 feet, it has disappeared. These colors are followed in their disappearance by yellow, green, blue, indigo and violet. Light is so low at 600 feet down that photosynthesis has stopped. The total absence of light occurs at about 1,800 feet.

The dissipation of light and color in our underwater world has a lot to do with the survival of many marine creatures, especially smaller ones. There is one simple law in the oceans—big fish eat little fish. If a little fish can blend in with its surroundings, it has a much better chance of surviving. With the colors red, orange, and yellow removed from the light spectrum at shallow depths, brightly colored creatures that would appear red under a dive light are black in their natural surroundings. Orange creatures appear brown, and yellow creatures appear light brown.

So, to see the true colors of marine creatures, use a dive light. Shine the light on the reef three or four feet ahead of you. The light beam will bring out a great spectrum of colors on creatures of the deep. Seemingly muted–colored fish, sponges, anemones, corals, flatworms, segmented worms, bryozoans, shellfish, crustaceans, sea stars and nudibranches now stand out color-coded against other marine formations of completely different colors. Without artificial lighting, many species might go unnoticed.

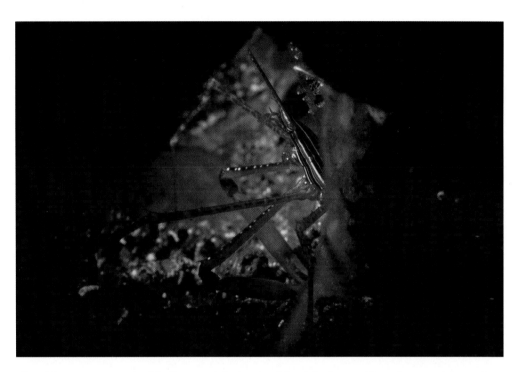

Good buoyancy control is the most important part in preventing damage to coral reefs. It is best to view small marine creatures like this arrow crab by allowing one's feet and legs to float perpendicular to the reef's surface. W

Some divers say by shining a light on a fish or other marine creature you startle them and cause them to randomly flee and crash into crevice walls or into the jaws of a larger fish. This is rarely the case. Dive lights do not seem to reveal their presence to predators or make them more susceptible to being eaten when you swim away. Dive lights do not even seem to affect mating and reproduction behavior. Nature's creatures have evolved in such a way that these important biological processes often seem to have built-in safeguards. Scientists have found it takes several weeks of continuous light to affect a change. A major exception in marine life are sea turtles, which are very sensitive to light when females are hauling out on a beach to lay eggs or when their hatchlings are scrambling to the oceans.

Handling marine creatures

On occasions, divers have been known to take a variety of foods ranging from dinner scraps to spry cans of cheese to feed fish. Once back on board the boat they exclaim "wasn't that great" or "did you see all those fish!" They should know better.

Feeding fish is no different than feeding any other wild animal. The short-term pleasures we receive from our selfish actions are not worth the long-term effects on wild creatures. Feeding fish used to be a popular pastime for many divers. It still is with some, but thanks to an influx of educational information in today's diving journals, most divers are becoming more ecologically minded and understand that their actions affect the marine environment.

Some divers handle marine creatures in an attempt to get great photographs. Before you touch or move any marine creature, ask yourself if an image is worth a possible loss of a life. If we move a sea horse, nudibranch or other smaller creature from its hiding space to an area that is more photogenic, open and easier to photograph in, we are endangering the creature's life.

From out of the murky depths glides a giant plankton-eating mantaray. W

Even if we are gentle, take our time and gently move subjects we wish to photograph, we are causing them major stress. By moving them out from hiding into a more open area, we are exposing them to the very real danger of being eaten. "Proper techniques" for moving small marine creatures are being taught today, but such practices are frowned upon because of their cumulative effects worldwide. When we reach into, move, or put back a small marine creature, we often unknowingly damage the marine life surrounding a creature. Reefs are very sensitive. They are complex living, breathing, growing colonies of organisms, not hard, sharp pieces of calcium as commonly perceived. The hard stuff is only their outer shells. Inside, countless living organisms are interdependently building a reef community.

Handling any small marine organism has a real potential of physically damaging and harming that creature. What we consider gentle might not be gentle to a creature 1/100th of our size.

For example, being puffed up is not the norm for pufferfish or porcupinefish. Only if they are being harassed do these fish inflate, and rarely so even then. Inflated puffers look great for pictures, but it takes a lot of effort on behalf of a diver to get one to inflate. Inflation is a self-defense technique utilized by these fish to avoid being eaten. They inflate only after trying to flee and have no other recourse. Inflated fish become slower and more vulnerable to larger predators, because they have wasted valuable energy inflating themselves. Once puffers are inflated, it takes a considerably longer time for them to deflate.

For purely selfish reasons, divers should be wary of pufferfish and porcupinefish. They have powerful jaws with buckteeth good for biting fingers.

Sharks

There are about 370 species of sharks worldwide, and sharks have been around for some 300 million years. Still, they are misunderstood. They are portrayed as

*Well hidden in its natural surrounding, this black fish appears bright red under artificial lighting.*W

bloodthirsty killing machines, but you have a better chance of winning the lottery or getting struck by lightning than you do of getting attacked by a shark. Reality, however, does not sell as many newspapers and movie tickets as sensationalism. Sharks, like most wild animals, can be dangerous, especially when they are feeding, but their behavior has been greatly overdramatized, and they have often been abused.

Sharks are efficient, well-adapted predators that keep ocean ecosystems in balance. For countless millennia, they have ruled the deep, but today, due primarily to overfishing, shark populations have dropped and many species are in danger of extinction. Sharks are being harvested to make a delicacy known as shark fin soup, and their fins can bring as much as $200 per pound in Asian markets. A consumption-oriented, short-sighted market is diminishing not only the populations of fish worldwide but the fishing industry itself.

Sharks are curious creatures, and if an opportunity is presented properly they will come in close to get a good look at a diver. Photographing a school of 250 hammerhead sharks is an unforgettable adventure.

Sharks do not like diver's bubbles or vertical divers; most marine creatures swim horizontally and do not bubble. If you see a shark in the distance and would like to get closer or have it get closer to you, orient yourself horizontally near the bottom and hum through your regulator so you produce small unnoticeable bubbles. Direct eye contact often will make a shark turn away. Turn your camera aside, because the lens looks like an eye. When the shark is close enough, turn to get a good look and to take your picture.

While it is rarely a problem to swim with sharks, never enter open water with sharks that are feeding or being feed.

Marine mammals

Since man began to sail the oceans, marine mammals have fascinated us. The

The sand tiger shark has an undeserved reputation as a vicious predator based on its appearance. Some 300 million years in the making, this shark is now endangered in many parts of the world. C

gentle giants that rise to the ocean's surface, catch a breath of air and then descend to unknown depths have generated fables and stories throughout history. Marine mammals have been thought of as monsters and mermaids and worshiped as gods and demons. We all want to see and get close to these marvelous creatures.

Whale watching is a fast-growing industry. Millions of people enjoy searching for these elusive air-breathing, deep-diving mammals. In Florida, people gather to watch manatees. Dolphins following boats excite tourists just as they did sailors in times of old who considered them good omens.

Even though we enjoy having sea lions, seals, manatees and whales come up to investigate us, it is illegal for us to swim after, chase,and touch marine mammals. It is not, however, illegal to be in the water and have one swim up to you. Illegal or not, the harassment of any animal is the fastest way to have them leave you.

Marine mammals are highly intelligent creatures and have sophisticated senses that can detect a diver, snorkeler or a boat approaching long before we get close enough to see them. If a whale rises off in the distance, laws restrict how close you can approach. They may approach a boat with its engine off if you are not aggressive, loud and unruly—and if you are lucky. Some whale species, such as humpbacks and orcas, breach or jump out of the water and are best observed from a distance.

In areas where sea lions and seals are not harassed, they appear playful and are a joy to view and photograph.

Marine reptiles

Sea turtles are true marine reptiles. These rare and graceful creatures are native to warm waters throughout the world and sometimes can be seen when you are diving. If you wish to see a sea turtle up close while underwater, approach it directly from behind and be careful to stay there where it cannot see you. Never reach out and touch a turtle. Once you

The dolphin is an intelligent marine mammal, and if not harassed, they may approach divers in the wild. C

have enjoyed your visit with the turtle, stay directly behind it until the turtle is at least 10 feet away, so you do not startle it as you leave the area.

All of the world's sea turtles need our help protecting nest beachcs, preventing entanglements in shrimp nets and fishing line, and halting the dumping of plastic bags and balloons. If the turtles swallow the plastic, it will block their digestive systems, and they will starve.

The marine environment is a fascinating, mysterious world. It remains relatively unknown and unexplored, a world filled with answers awaiting our discoveries. As environmentally friendly divers, we must do our best to protect this fragile ecosystem. It is our obligation as divers to take only pictures and to leave only bubbles.

Everybody thinks you need to be in warm water to see colorful marine creatures. These brightly colored sea anemones are found in the cold water of the Pacific Northwest C

Jet Ski Habits

Jet skis can travel down small narrow streams and over shallow water mud flats. They can go where no man or woman has gone before—and at great speeds. Their turbulent propulsion churns up delicate shallow-water habitats. Their noise, stream of airborne water, and crashing wakes disturb wildlife.

Of all reported marine accidents in 1994 involving motorized watercraft, more than 70 percent involved jet skis.

For the protection of wetland habitats and wildlife and for the safety of jet skiers, please follow these guidelines:

- Avoid streams that are too narrow for a typical motorboat.

- Treat streams narrower than 50 feet as no-wake zones.

- Avoid water shallower than three feet. These areas are the most sensitive marine habitats and potentially dangerous if a skier were to fall.

- Maintain a distance of at least 100 feet from the edge of marshlands.

- Slow down and produce no wake when passing canoes and kayaks.

- Avoid all swimming areas by at least 100 feet.

- Never try to outrun a moving motorboat.

- Obey all motorboat laws; jet skis are not exempted from such regulations.

- Use your brain, not the throttle, to control your jet ski.

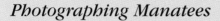
Photographing Manatees

The manatee is a harmless, gentle, plant-eating marine mammal found primarily in the warmer coastal rivers and waters of Florida. When swimming, boating, or diving in Florida's inland waterways, take caution not to endanger the lives of the West Indian manatees, which are protected by both federal and state laws.

The Marine Mammal Protection Act of 1972 and the Endangered Species Act of 1973 make it illegal to harass, capture, or kill any marine mammal—including the manatee. In addition, the Florida Manatee Sanctuary Act states: "It is unlawful for any person, at any time, by any means, intentionally or negligently, to annoy, molest, harass, or disturb any manatee."

The following guidelines allow manatees to be photographed and observed and water activities to be accomplished without violating the provisions of these three laws. These guidelines are designed to help you better understand the regulations and help you have a memorable experience while still protecting manatees. A good rule of thumb when interacting or photographing manatees is to remain passive and not harass them. Harassment is defined as any activity that alters their natural behavior, including:

- Approaching a manatee before the animal first approaches or touches you.

- Actively pursuing/chasing/swimming after or cornering a manatee while swimming or diving.

- Poking, probing, stabbing a manatee at any time with an object including but not limited to close-up frames or a person's hands or feet.

- Any activity that would separate or single out an individual from a group.

- Any activity that would separate a cow from her calf or a calf from a cow.

- Any attempt to snag, hook, position, hold, grab, pinch, or ride a manatee.

- Any attempt to feed a manatee; feeding conditions them to come toward the sound of an outboard motor and increases the chances for a boat or prop strike.

Do not enter designated/posted sanctuaries for any reason!

Theodore Ondler
Assistant Refuge Manager
Chassahowitzka National Wildlife Refuge

"If you understand, things are just as they are; if you do not understand, things are just as they are."

Zen Verse

*About
the Author*

*Bill Hartley teaching the refinements of photography to
local students in Africa. Bill is the one with the beard.* W

William W. Hartley has been pursuing a career as a photo-biologist since receiving his degree in natural resources from the University of Rhode Island. As a lecturer, author, photographer, and tour leader, Bill has been an international advocate of viewing and photographing wildlife without causing harm to habitat or stress on animals. He has bought his message to thousands of people.

A native of New Jersey, Bill resides with his wife, Marleen, and their children, Jacqueline and William, among the pine barrens along the seacoast that first instilled in him his love for nature.

Index

Numbers in italics refer to photographs;
NP=national park.

Suggested Reading

Sharing Nature With Children
 Joseph Bharat Cornell

The Earth Speaks
 Steve VanMatre & Bill Weiler

Wildlife Photography
 Joe McDonald

Landscape Photography
 John Shaw

Galapagos
 Paul Humann

The Kingdom
 Art Wolfe & Douglas Chadwick

Our Endangered Parks
 From Foghorn Press

How I Photograph Wildlife and Nature
 Leonard Lee Rue III

Beyond The Basics
 George Lepp

Guide To Bird and Nature Photography
 Laurie Campbell

Photographing the Patterns of Nature
 Gary Braasch

Rodale's Scuba Diving Magazine

Photo Traveler Journal

New Titles From Partnership Press

Fall '96	**The Young Photographer** Basic basics (juvenile)
Spring '97	**Hooked on Fishing** A beginners guide (juvenile)
Fall '97	**Introducing Your Children to Nature and Wildlife** (adult/ juvenile)
Spring '98	**The Traveler** A guide to going places and taking great travel photographs (adult)

Partnership Press™
P.O. Box 1156, Tuckerton, NJ 08087
Phone: 609-296-6827   Fax: 609-296-1682

Special Ordering Information

You can order autographed copies of *Loving Nature ...the right way* or autographed museum quality prints (Ilfochrome or Cibachrome Prints) of any photograph from this book. These can be great gifts for holidays, birthdays, anniversaries or that special up-coming trip.

Autograph book to: *Special Note:*

_____   _____

_____   _____

_____   _____

Quantity:	Title	Unit Price in U.S. $	Total
_____	Loving Nature	$19.95	_____

Autographed print: page no. _____
Description _____
___8x10   ___14x16   ___24x36   ___30x40
$60. ea. $120. ea. $250. ea. $350. ea.   Total _____

Autographed print: page no. _____
Description _____
___8x10   ___14x16   ___24x36   ___30x40
$60. ea. $120. ea. $250. ea. $350. ea.   Total _____

Shipping, Handling and Insurance
   Add $3.95 for every purchase up to $50.00
   and $1.00 for every $20.00 thereafter   Total _____
New Jersey residents add 6% sales tax   Total _____
                                        Total Payment _____

Ship To:
Name:_____Phone: _____
Street address: _____
City:_____ State:_____Zip Code: ____

Orders must be prepaid by one of the following methods:
_____ Check or money order
_____ Bill Charge Card _____ Visa_____ Master card
       Name as it appears on card:_____
       Card #_____Exp. Date_____
       Authorized Signature_____

Mail orders to:
Partnership Press™, P.O. Box 1156, Tuckerton, NJ 08087
Phone: 609-296-6827   Fax: 609-296-1682

Field
Notes

Field
Notes

Field
Notes

Field
Notes

Field
Notes